Investigation into the Origin and Character of Surficial Sedimentary Deposits at the Midshore Regional Solid Waste Facility near Easton, Maryland

By Joseph P. Smoot, Wayne L. Newell, and Benjamin D. DeJong

Open-File Report 2009–1052

U.S. Department of the Interior
U.S. Geological Survey

U.S. Department of the Interior
KEN SALAZAR, Secretary

U.S. Geological Survey
Suzette M. Kimball, Acting Director

U.S. Geological Survey, Reston, Virginia: 2009

For product and ordering information:
World Wide Web: http://www.usgs.gov/pubprod
Telephone: 1-888-ASK-USGS

For more information on the USGS—the Federal source for science about the Earth,
its natural and living resources, natural hazards, and the environment:
World Wide Web: http://www.usgs.gov
Telephone: 1-888-ASK-USGS

Contents

Figures

Table

Conversion Factors

Multiply	By	To obtain
Length		
centimeter (cm)	0.3937	inch (in.)
millimeter (mm)	0.03937	inch (in.)
meter (m)	3.281	foot (ft)
kilometer (km)	0.6214	mile (mi)
kilometer (km)	0.5400	mile, nautical (nmi)
meter (m)	1.094	yard (yd)
inch (in.)	2.54	centimeter (cm)
inch (in.)	25.4	millimeter (mm)
foot (ft)	0.3048	meter (m)
mile (mi.)	1.609	kilometer (km)

Investigation into the Origin and Character of Surficial Sedimentary Deposits at the Midshore Regional Solid Waste Facility near Easton, Maryland

By Joseph P. Smoot, Wayne L. Newell, and Benjamin D. DeJong

Abstract

A temporary exposure at the Midshore Regional Solid Waste Facility near Easton, MD, provided an opportunity to document the characteristics of the complex assemblage of surficial facies in that area. This unusually large cross section allowed interpretation of the changing processes that shaped the landscape in response to climate change through the late Pleistocene. Eight stratigraphic units were recognized: (1) gray, fossiliferous, muddy silt of the marine Miocene Choptank Formation; (2) coarse, crossbedded conglomerate of the late Miocene to Pliocene fluvial Pensauken Formation; (3) bioturbated muddy conglomerate interpreted as deposits of small colluvial fans; (4) pebbly, quartzose sand overlying a planar erosional surface reflecting a marine transgression; (5) irregular pods and lenses of sand and gravel deformed into bowl-shaped folds and faulted, which are interpreted as wind deposits over a semipermanent snow cover (niveo-aeolian deposits); (6) crossbedded sand and conglomerate with abundant mud partings indicating tidal influences on sinuous stream channels; (7) heavily bioturbated silt and sand with abundant root casts and flattened vesicles interpreted as aeolian loess deposits in marshy fens; and (8) pebbly sand and mud with scattered boulders and cobbles that reflect modern infill of the excavation by the operators. Soils formed on units 3, 4, and 7. Superimposed on units 4, 5, and 7 is evidence of deep freezing and permafrost development and subsequent thermokarst development after thawing, which includes large, complexly filled wedge-shaped cracks, deformed bedding and faults, fluid-injection structures, and spherical blobs of sand and mud. Each of the stratigraphic units has irregular distributions and lateral changes. The results of this study provide a unique insight into the geometry of surficial deposits that will help facilitate mapping of units, interpretation of cored intervals, and understanding of ground-penetrating radar profiles. The study also documents the widespread effects of permafrost during the last glacial episode well south of the maximum advance of ice sheets.

Introduction

The U.S. Geological Survey (USGS) is currently mapping the distribution of Mid-Atlantic Coastal Plain surficial deposits in the mid-Chesapeake Bay region. The maps will provide important information for land-use planning, ground-water recharge modeling, and estimating the distribution of economic materials such as sand and gravel. The mapping also provides important information on climate change through the late Quaternary and insights on geomorphic response to changes in sea level. This report provides a sedimentary description of a rare, large vertical exposure of these surficial deposits. The study area is a borrow pit for cover at the Midshore Regional Solid Waste Facility near Easton in Talbot County, MD (fig. 1). The exposure provides some sense of the three-dimensional geometry of sedimentary facies, which allows interpretation of depositional processes through several different climatic settings. The information afforded by the studies at this exposure site is critical in forming the description of various surficial geologic map units and the interpretation of auger and core holes drilled at strategic locations to support the geologic map.

Talbot County is situated east of the Chesapeake Bay and north and west of the Choptank River. The western part of the county adjacent to Chesapeake Bay occupies low terraces underlain by the Quaternary Kent Island Formation (Owens and Denny, 1979). These low terraces are bounded to the east by the Princess Anne Scarp, which is cut into a central north-south-trending upland.

Another sequence of terraces, mostly estuarine, occurs to the east and south of the central upland and is bounded in turn by the Choptank River. The terrace deposits unconformably overlie the Miocene Choptank Formation, a marine shelf deposit exposed along bluffs of the Choptank River. Near the study site, river-bluff exposures of thick fossil beds are the type section of zone 17 of the Choptank Formation (Shattuck, 1902).

The central uplands are underlain by the Choptank Formation and the overlying, but unconformable, Pensauken Formation (Owens and Denny, 1979). The Pensauken Formation is a fluvial to deltaic gravel that is many tens of meters thick and is late Micocene to Pliocene in age.

Overlying gravel of the Pensauken Formation in the uplands, and overlying the lower terrace deposits inset into the uplands, is a ubiquitous cover of mixed dune sands, slope deposits, and discontinuous fluvial deposits called the Parsonsburg Sand (Denny and others, 1979). The Parsonsburg Sand geomorphology includes distinctive dune forms having 1 to 3 meters (m) of relief (Denny and Owens, 1979), closed basins, and elliptical, raised-rim, ephemeral ponds with peat and perched water tables. The Parsonsburg Sand and its geomorphology have been dated, yielding a range from ~ 30 ka to 13 ka (30,000 to 13,000 years before present; Denny and others, 1979).

Across Talbot County, outcrops are rare. Bluffs are commonly covered with colluvium and vegetation. Excavations are ephemeral, and exposed bluffs along the terrace margins are often short lived after erosion during large storms. Furthermore, it is increasingly common for areas of bluff exposures to be protected by engineering structures. The ephemeral exposures afforded by the Midshore Regional Solid Waste Facility are invaluable for defining the stratigraphy of surficial deposits and the underlying Miocene sediments and for interpreting details of the history of landform development in Talbot County. The surficial geology presented here provides the following: (1) details of the shallow-shelf, sulfide-rich and fossiliferous beds of the Choptank Formation (Zones 17–20 of Shattuck, 1902), (2) a description of the unconformable Pensauken Formation, the major source of Pleistocene slope deposits and lag gravels of the Pleistocene estuarine terraces, (3) details of terrace stratigraphy and sedimentology that provide insight into sea-level high stands and lowering, (4) details of cold-climate surface modifications during the last glacial maximum (LGM, about 21,000 years before present), including windblown and slope deposits and structures formed by freezing and thawing of the sediment cover, and (5) the framework for Holocene terrestrial deposits, including swamps, alluvium, and legacy sediments. This report is the first in a series of detailed descriptions of ephemeral exposures and ground-penetrating radar (GPR) profiles that will be integrated into surficial geologic map units and the interpretation of landscape evolution in the Chesapeake Bay region.

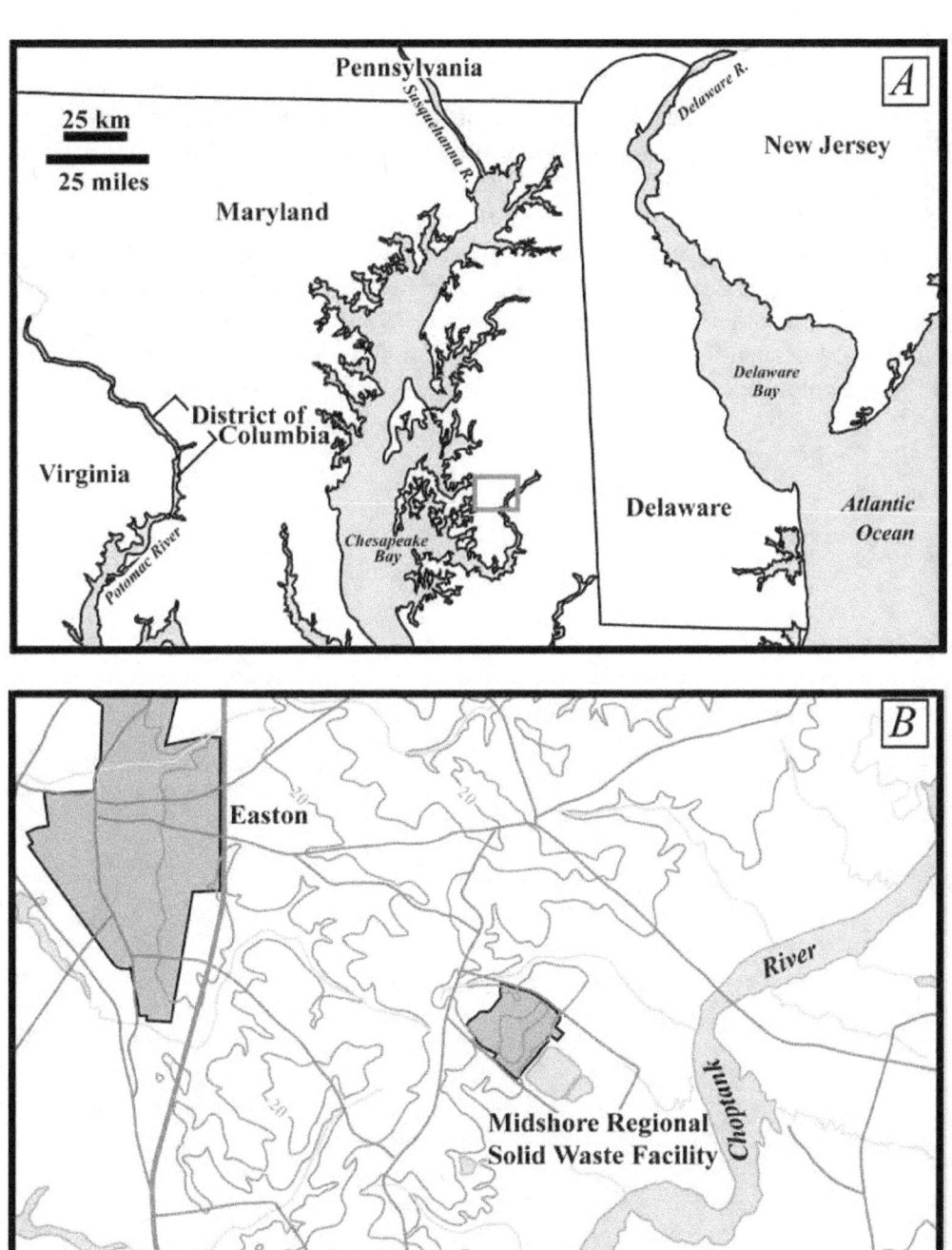

Figure 1. Location maps of the study site on the Delmarva Peninsula. *A*, General map of Delmarva Peninsula in vicinity of study area (red box). *B*, Map of area outlined by red box in figure 1*A* showing location of Easton, MD, and the Midshore Regional Solid Waste Facility (gray areas). Major roads (red) and elevation contours (10-meter intervals) are shown. Modified from http://www.midshoresolidwaste.com.

Study Site

The Midshore Regional Solid Waste Facility has provided sanitary disposal of trash and other solid-waste material for Queen Anne's, Caroline, and Talbot Counties in Maryland since 1991 and Kent County in Delaware since 1992. The site is scheduled to close in 2011 when a new site will open in Caroline County. The pit used in this study was dug on the northeastern edge of the property (fig. 2) to provide sediment to cover mounds of solid waste. The pit was dug into the southern edge of a topographic high terrace bounding the valley of the Choptank River to the east (fig. 1). The pit cuts through a terrace mapped as the Kent Island 15-foot terrace (Owens and Denny, 1986). The pit provided (1) a continuous exposure trending northwest perpendicular to the topographic high that is about 600 m long and 2 to 3.5 m high, and (2) some discontinuous exposures west of the main wall ranging from 1 to 2 m in height.

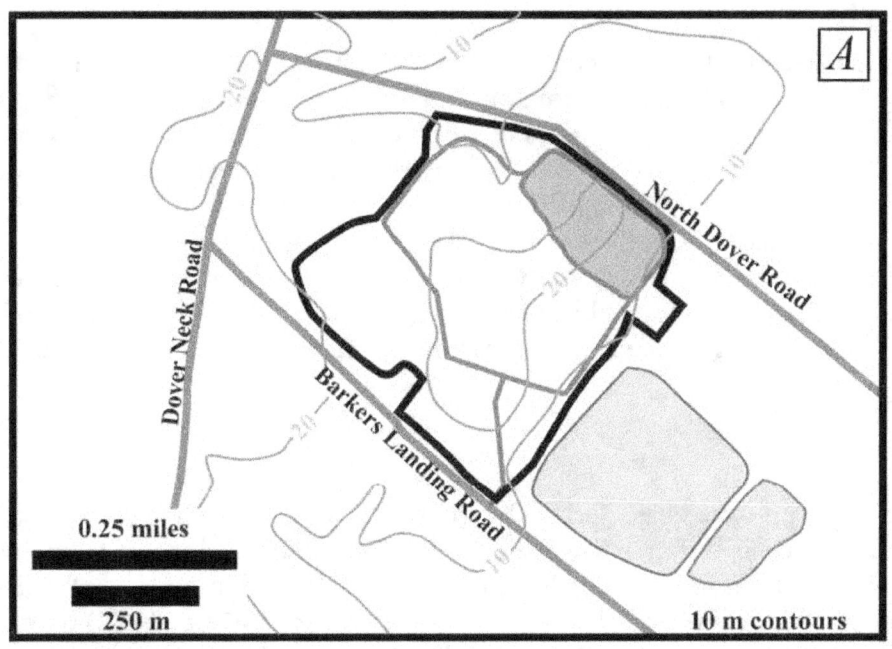

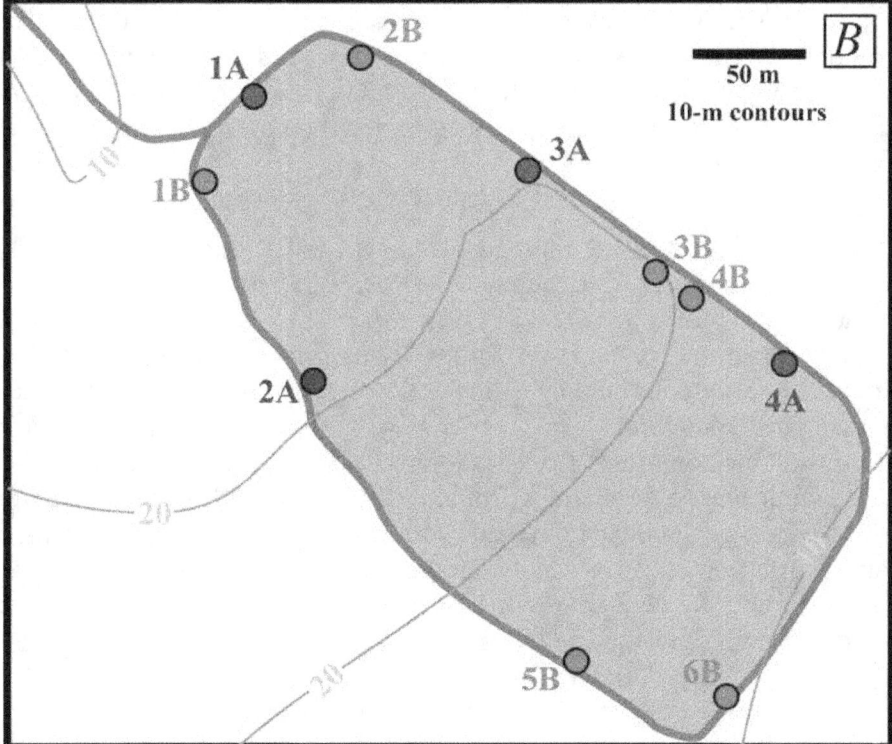

Figure 2. Detailed maps of the study site showing the location of the Midshore Regional Solid Waste Facility, the pit studied, and sites where photographs were taken. *A*, Location of the Midshore Regional Solid Waste Facility (black outline) and the pit studied (gray area). Major roads (red), dirt roads (purple), and 10-meter contours (orange) are shown. *B*, The pit studied (gray area) and surrounding dirt roads (purple). Locations of sites where the surface was cleaned and photographed include 2007 sites (1A–4A, blue circles) and 2008 sites (1B–6B, red circles). Click on a site (except 6B) to link to a photograph.

Wayne Newell and Ben DeJong first viewed the site in 2007. It was subsequently visited five times by the authors in the spring and summer of 2008 to establish the lateral relationships of the observed facies. Because of continuous excavation, the exposed faces of the pit shifted over that time period and are only approximately known from the earlier visit. Weathered material and wall collapse were removed with pick and shovel from 3- to 4-m-wide sections of the pit wall, exposing about 3 m of vertical section. Digging marks were scraped from shoveled surfaces using a knife. The surfaces were then photographed and logged in detail. One locality was sampled for analysis in the lab, but exposures were inadvertently destroyed before the other localities were sampled and before all lateral relationships could be fully verified. The approximate locations of described sites are labeled on figure 2 and referenced throughout the text.

Stratigraphy

Sediments exposed in the pit were characterized by grain size, color, assemblage of sedimentary structures, and the nature of contacts between units. The lateral extent of units was ascertained by either walking out contacts or tracing them from photographic mosaics. The pit section consists of eight major units, listed in order of deposition: (1) gray, sulfide-rich, silty mud with sand interbeds, (2) orange-stained sand and gravel, (3) mottled green and orange sandy mud with beds of pebble gravel grading to sand, (4) pale-gray to pale-brown quartz sand, in places orange stained, containing scattered small pebbles, (5) deformed beds of orange-stained pebble gravels and white granule-rich sand, (6) brownish sand and gravel with silt and clay partings, (7) predominantly buff to pale-gray silt and fine orangish sand, and (8) mostly brown mixed sand, mud, and gravel. These units are described in detail below.

Unit 1

Unit 1 consists of silty mud with fine sand interbeds. Dark-gray silty mud that is rich in black monosulfide minerals makes up the floor of the pit and the lower part of some pit walls (fig. 3). Exposures of the mud show intervals with fine to medium sand layers making up thick laminae that are graded over an irregular scour base (fig. 3B) or that thicken and thin with wavy internal stratification (fig. 3D). Randomly oriented cylindrical features are defined by fillings of both sand and mud (fig. 3B and 3D). Casts of mollusk shells are visible on some broken surfaces (fig. 3C). The upper 30 to 40 centimeters (cm) below the upper contact of this unit are commonly brown to orange and structureless (fig. 3A).

Unit 1 is interpreted as the Miocene Choptank Formation (Shattuck, 1902), which is mapped along Choptank River exposures and tributary channels in the area surrounding the pit. The Choptank Formation is mostly blue-gray silty mud with intervals of fine sand and intense concentrations of shelly material. The sand layers are consistent with storm wave deposition in an otherwise quiet-water setting. Intense bioturbation is also consistent with a shallow marine setting.

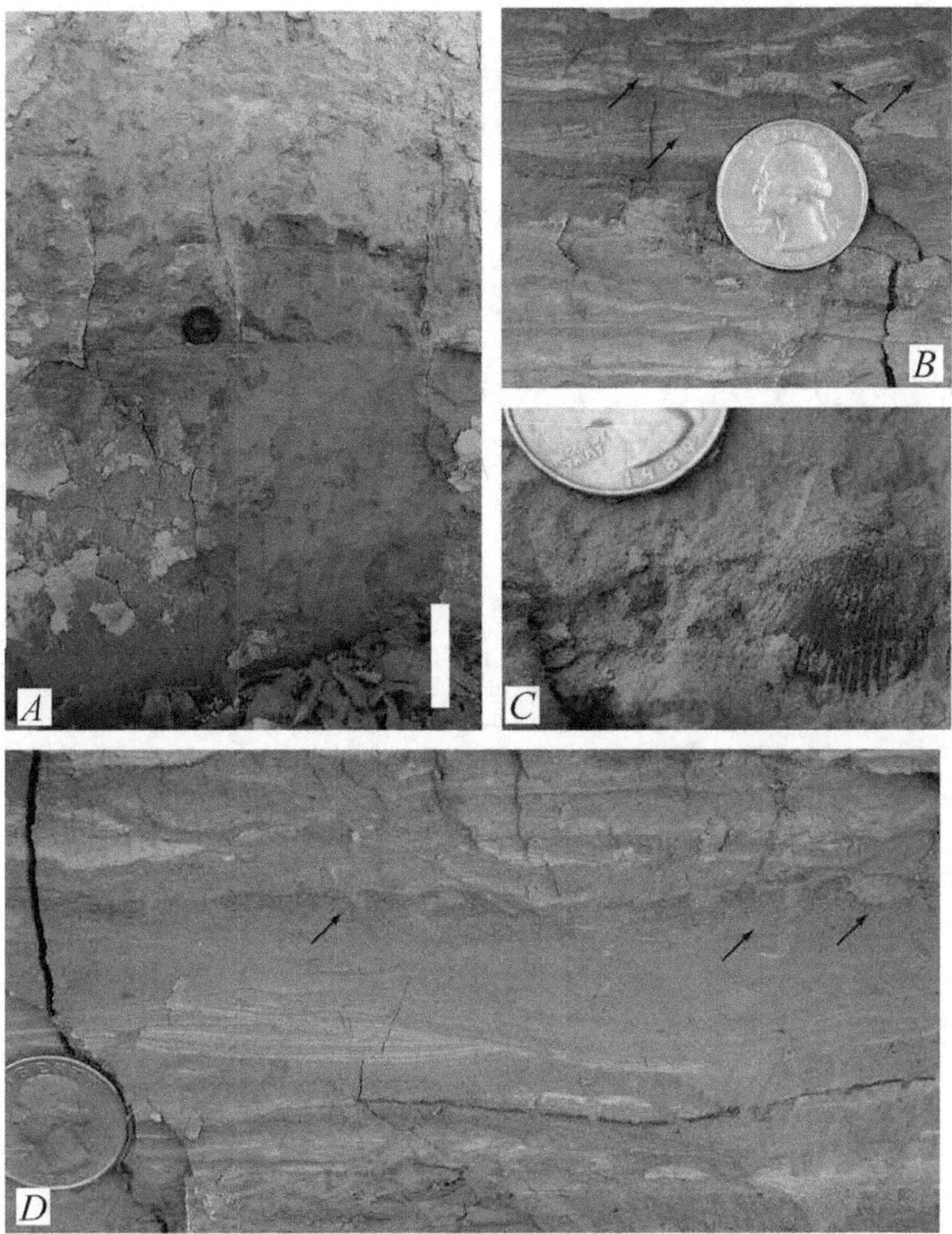

Figure 3. Photographs of unit 1 at site 2A showing typical gray mud, details of bedding and bioturbation, and a sediment cast of a mollusk shell. *A*, General view of section showing typical gray mud with brown and orange colors in the upper 30 cm. Scale bar is 20 cm long. *B*, Detail of bedding in unit 1 showing laminated coarse silt and very fine sand (light) alternating with muddy silt (dark). Ovate interruptions of the coarser layers are sediment-filled burrows (arrows). Coin is 2.5 cm in diameter. *C*, Sediment cast of a mollusk shell on a broken surface with a crust of iron sulfide minerals. Coin is 2.5 cm in diameter. *D*, Wavy bedding of very fine sand (light) indicating wave deposition. Note irregular light-gray projections into darker gray mud overlying the wavy bedding (arrows). These are sediment-filled burrows. Coin is 2.5 cm in diameter.

Unit 2

Orange-stained sand and gravel defined as unit 2 overlie unit 1 in all exposures in the pit. The contact is irregular, erosive, and overlain by cobble- and boulder-sized gravel (fig. 4). Goethite cement commonly produces one or two sheetlike indurated horizons a few centimeters thick within the lower 10 to 15 cm of this unit (fig. 4B). Boulders and cobbles at the base of this unit are poorly sorted but are clast supported. No obvious internal sedimentary structures are visible, but in some exposures, the clasts may exhibit imbrication or an asymmetric distribution of coarse material on one side of a clast (shadow fabric).

Overlying the contact, pebble conglomerate and pebbly sand commonly exhibit dune-scale (decimeter) crossbedding with trough and tabular stratification (fig. 5). The crossbeds typically decrease in scale upward on the scale of a meter or more within a section in progressively finer grained sediment. Trough crossbedding and shadow fabrics both indicate flow primarily to the south or southwest. Muddy sand containing scattered pebbles also occurs laterally and is truncated by lens-shaped sequences with crossbedding (fig. 5A).

Unit 2 is interpreted as the late Miocene to Pliocene Pensauken Formation (Owens and Denny, 1979). The Pensauken Formation is a fluvial to deltaic gravel that is rich in quartz, feldspar, and chert clasts and contains heavy minerals reflecting a source in the Appalachian Mountains. Both white and black chert pebbles were observed in the pit, as were a few clasts of reddish-brown siltstone that could be Triassic or Silurian rocks. The poorly developed upward-fining sequences that are dominated by dune-scale trough and tabular foresets are characteristic of braided-stream deposits. Channel thalwegs were floored with coarse material that trapped finer sediment during waning flood events, and dune-scale bedforms covered most of the channel floor during low-flow conditions. Midchannel bars produced the tabular-foreset sequences. Overbank areas within the braid plain were sites of mud accumulation between clasts and of intensive rooting and burrowing that destroyed any former stratification. The indurated goethite-rich horizons are interpreted as ground-water cements formed by the interaction of oxidized ground water flowing along the contact with the relatively impermeable, sulfide-rich unit 1.

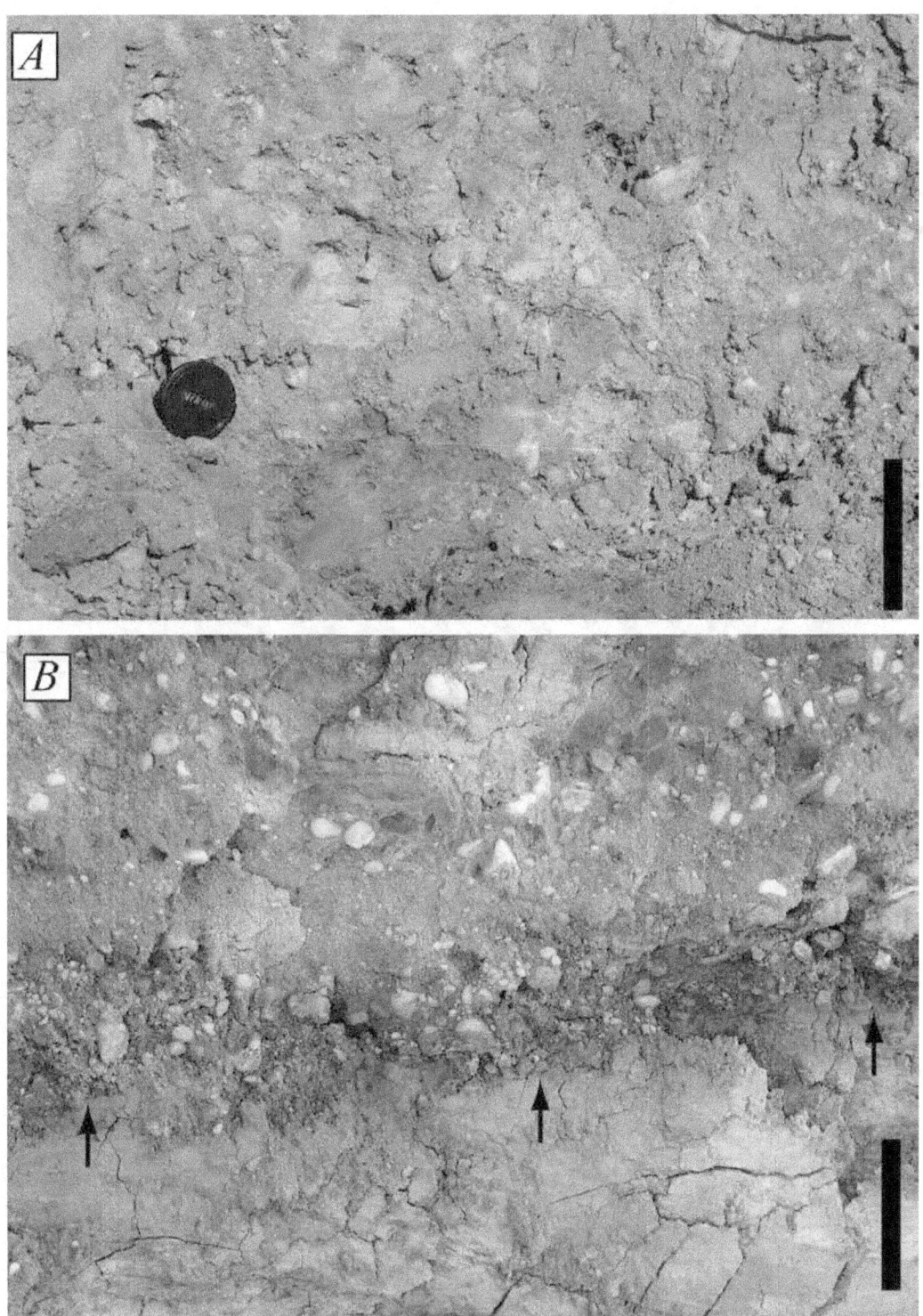

Figure 4. Photographs of unit 2 showing cobble conglomerate about 50 m southeast of site 4A and the contact between unit 1 and unit 2 at site 2B. *A*, Cobble conglomerate in low exposure about 50 m southeast of site 4A. Note weathered reddish blocks and overall poor sorting. Scale bar is 10 cm long. *B*, Contact between unit 1 and unit 2 (arrows) at site 2B. Segregation of coarse and fine layers reflects a large-scale trough crossbed. Note purplish goethite cement of conglomerate immediately overlying the contact. Scale bar is 15 cm long.

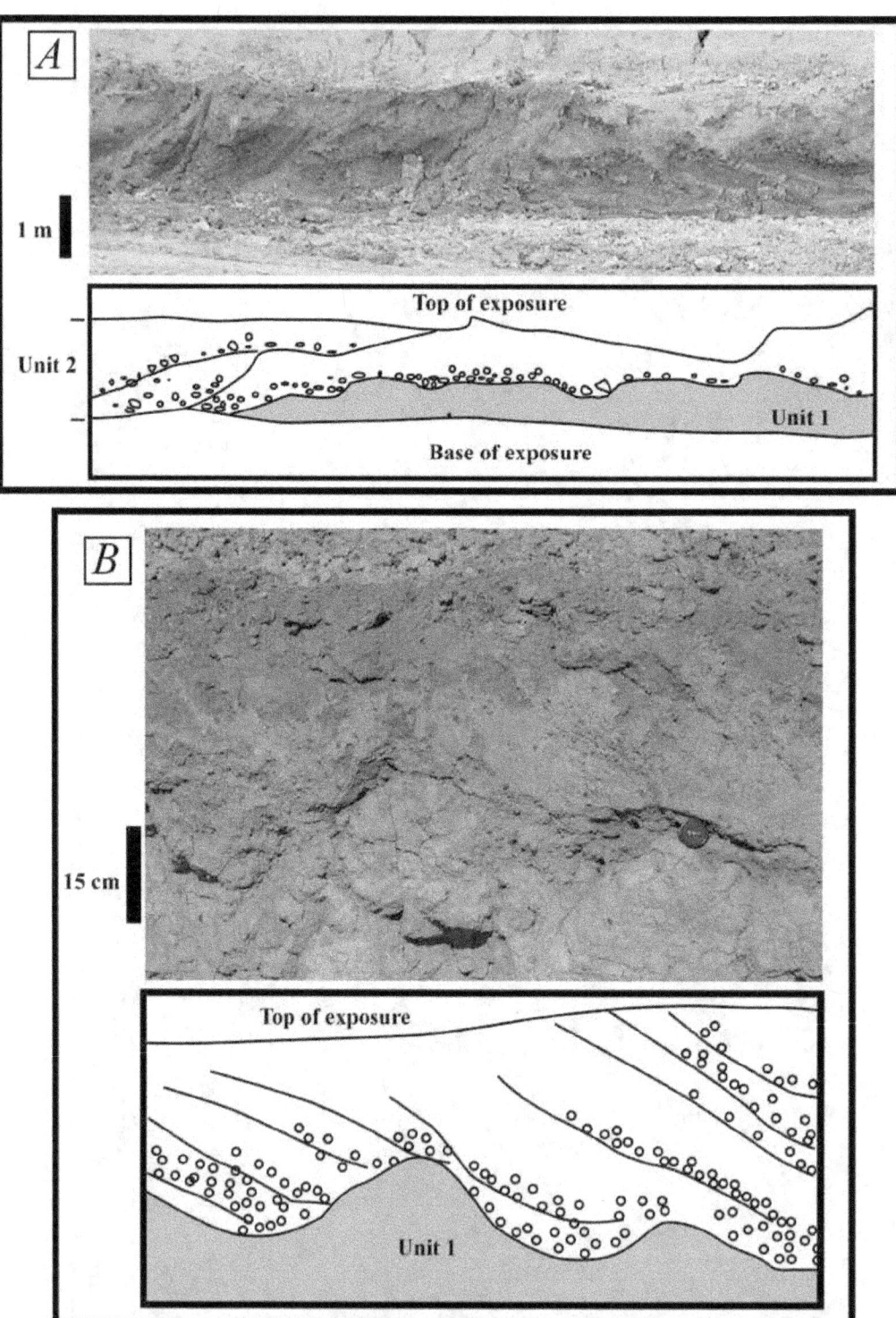

Figure 5. Photographs and sketches of unit 2 showing the contact between unit 1 and unit 2 near site 3A and about 50 m southeast of site 4A. *A,* General view of the contact between unit 1 and unit 2 along the northeastern wall of pit near site 3A. Note the relief of the contact and irregularity of boulder-cobble scour bases as shown in the sketch. The relief and irregularity are difficult to see in the photograph due to scrape marks made by heavy equipment and slough over the surface. *B,* Poorly exposed contact of unit 1 and unit 2 showing irregular contact and crossbedding. From low exposure about 50 m southeast of site 4A.

Unit 3

Unit 3 consists of mottled green and orange sandy mud with decimeter-scale beds of pebble gravel grading to sand (fig. 6). Unit 3 overlies unit 2 in most places, and the contact between the two units was poorly exposed in most places (fig. 7). The deposits appear to be less compact than the underlying Pensauken Formation, but the clasts are indistinguishable in character. Pebble gravel beds have sharp, relatively planar bases. The long axes of pebbles appear to be parallel to bedding, but there is no internal stratification (fig. 6B). The gravel and surrounding sandy mud are penetrated by ubiquitous cylindrical features mostly filled with sand and mud. Some of these are enhanced by a color difference with the surrounding sediment, but most are visible only where they contrast with the surrounding grain sizes or have preferential parting along the cylinder wall. Cylinder diameters range from about 2 cm to less than 1 millimeter (mm). No paleocurrent indicators were observed.

Unit 3 is interpreted as a younger fluvial deposit dominated by sediment fills of shallow, sheetlike channels that are overprinted by extensive soil development. It is possible that it represents a lateral facies of unit 2, but the consistent position over the typical unit 2 and the relatively lower degree of induration suggest a younger unit. The cylindrical features are interpreted as both root casts and burrows, but because of the sandy medium, clear distinctions are difficult to make. The color mottling of this unit may also indicate some soil development with a localized reducing condition superimposed on the oxidized sediment. The similarity in provenance to unit 2 is attributed to reworking of Pensauken Formation outcrops from the adjacent highland to the west.

Figure 6. Photographs of unit 3 showing mottled mud with pebble layers and sand-filled wedge at site 3B. *A,* Cross section of unit 3 at site 3B showing green- and orange-mottled mud with pebble layers. Vertical white feature is a sand-filled wedge attributed to permafrost. Scale bar is 50 cm long. *B,* Detail of area outlined by black box in figure 6*A.* Coarse sand and pebble layer in upper half shows no internal bedding or paleocurrent indication. Greenish mud in lower half has orange mottles. Sediment-filled tubes are abundant but are not visible in photograph. Scale bar is 10 cm long.

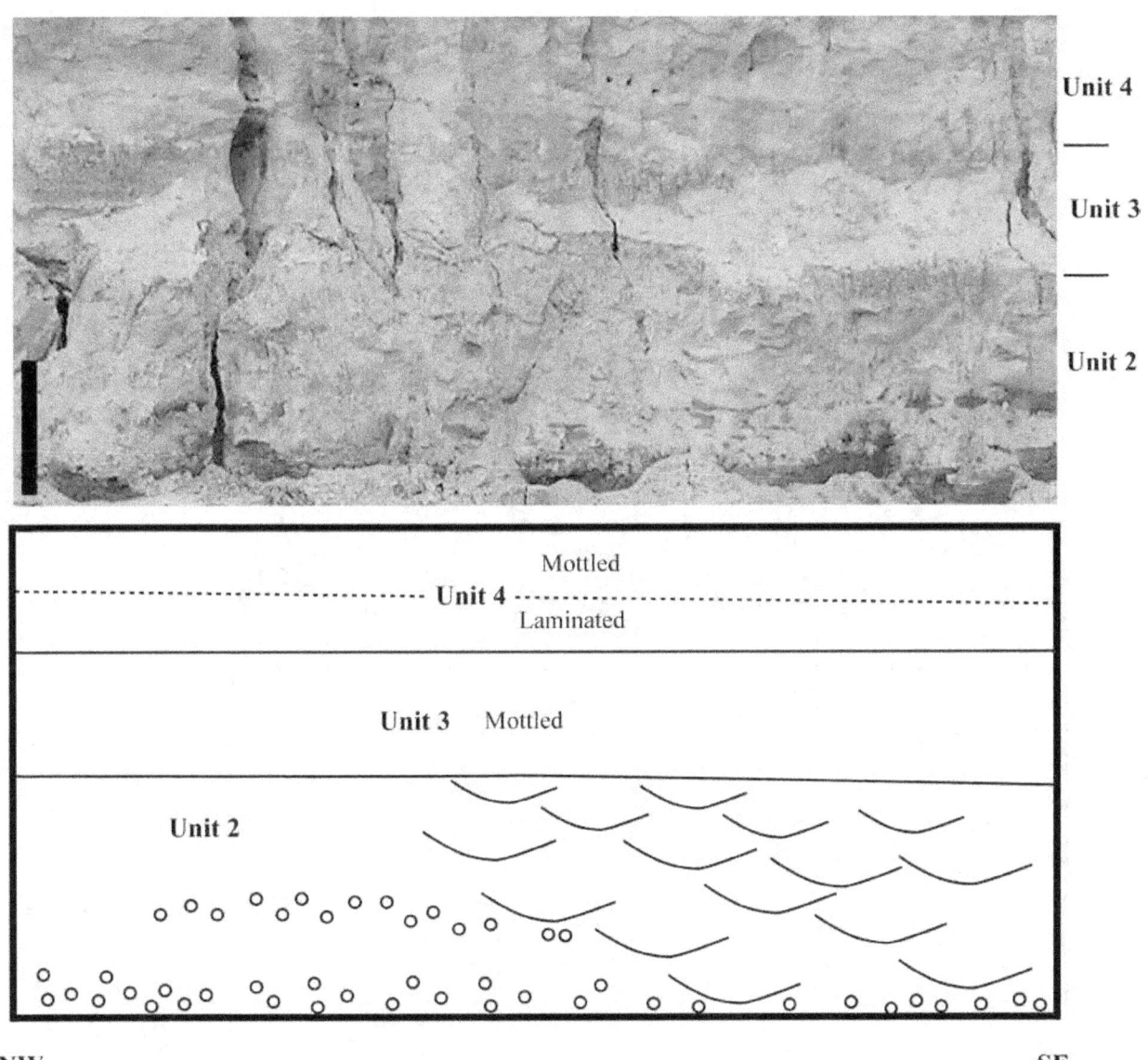

NW   SE

Figure 7. Photograph and sketch showing general view of contacts between units 2, 3, and 4 at an unprepared site just northwest of site 3A. Unit 2 contains numerous trough crossbeds with paleocurrent indicators to the south. Unit 3 is heavily mottled with abundant bioturbation features. Unit 4 includes a lower part that has planar lamination and an upper part that has mottling and bioturbation. Scale bar is 1 m long.

Unit 4

Unit 4 consists of pale-gray to pale-brown quartz sand, in places stained orange, which sharply caps unit 3 and locally directly overlies unit 2 (figs. 8 and 9). The basal contact of unit 4 is planar everywhere and is commonly inclined at grades that drop over a meter at lateral distances of less than 50 m. The sand in unit 4 is dominated by quartz and commonly contains quartz pebbles. The sand grains and pebbles are characteristically moderately well rounded and better sorted than the underlying units. In some places, the lower part of the sand displays internal planar lamination or may have alternating layers of lenticular to wavy coarse sand separated by finer sand (figs. 8 and 9).

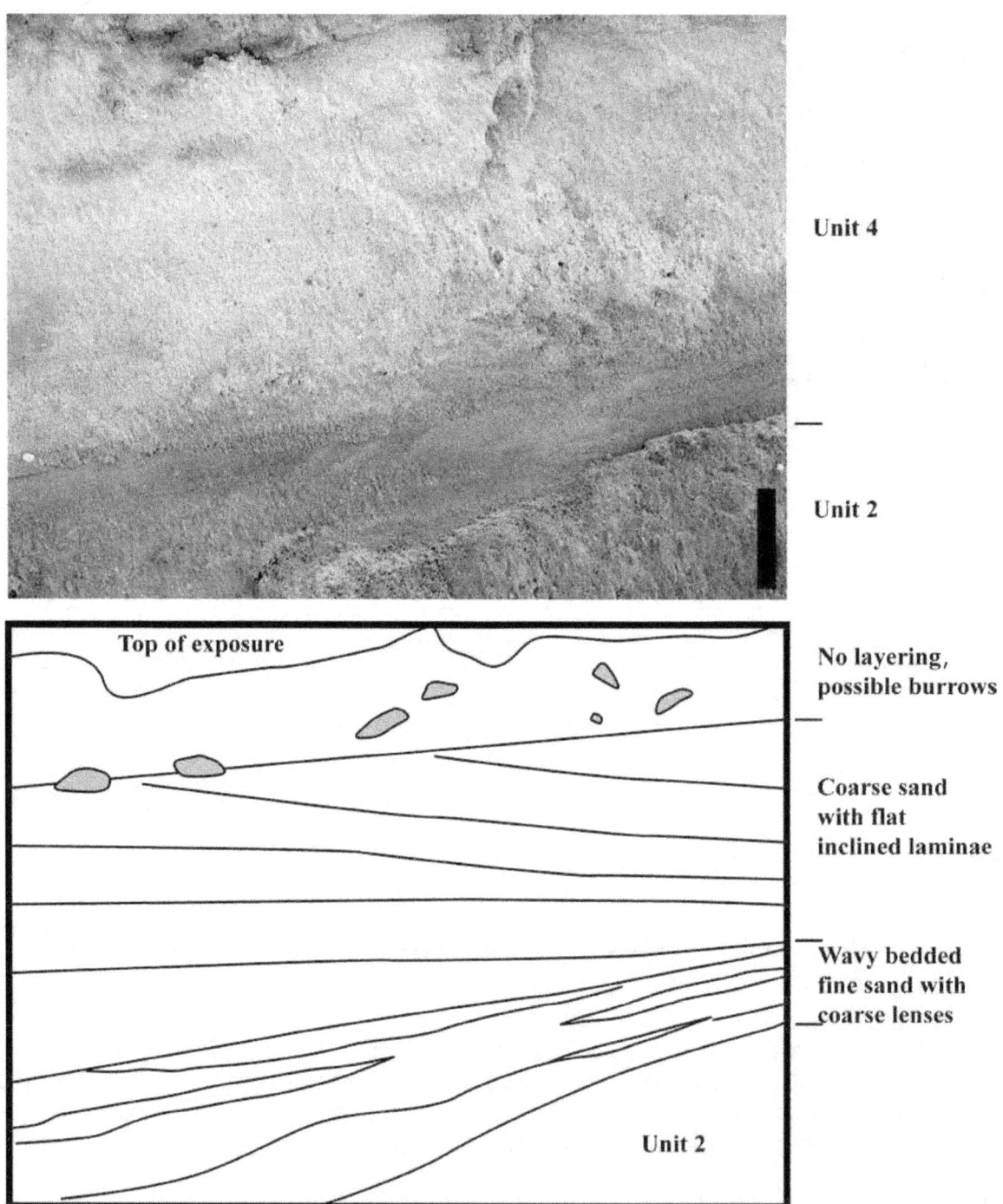

Figure 8. Photograph and sketch of the basal part of section at site 2B showing contact between unit 4 (above) and unit 2. Lowermost part of unit 4 consists of lenses of coarse sand within a fine sand suggesting wave ripples. The upper sand is more pebble rich and has faint, low-angle inclined laminae suggesting a beachfront environment. Upper part is disturbed by sediment-filled cylinders interpreted as burrows (gray in drawing). The upper contact of unit 4 was disturbed by heavy equipment in the pit. Scale bar is 15 cm long.

14

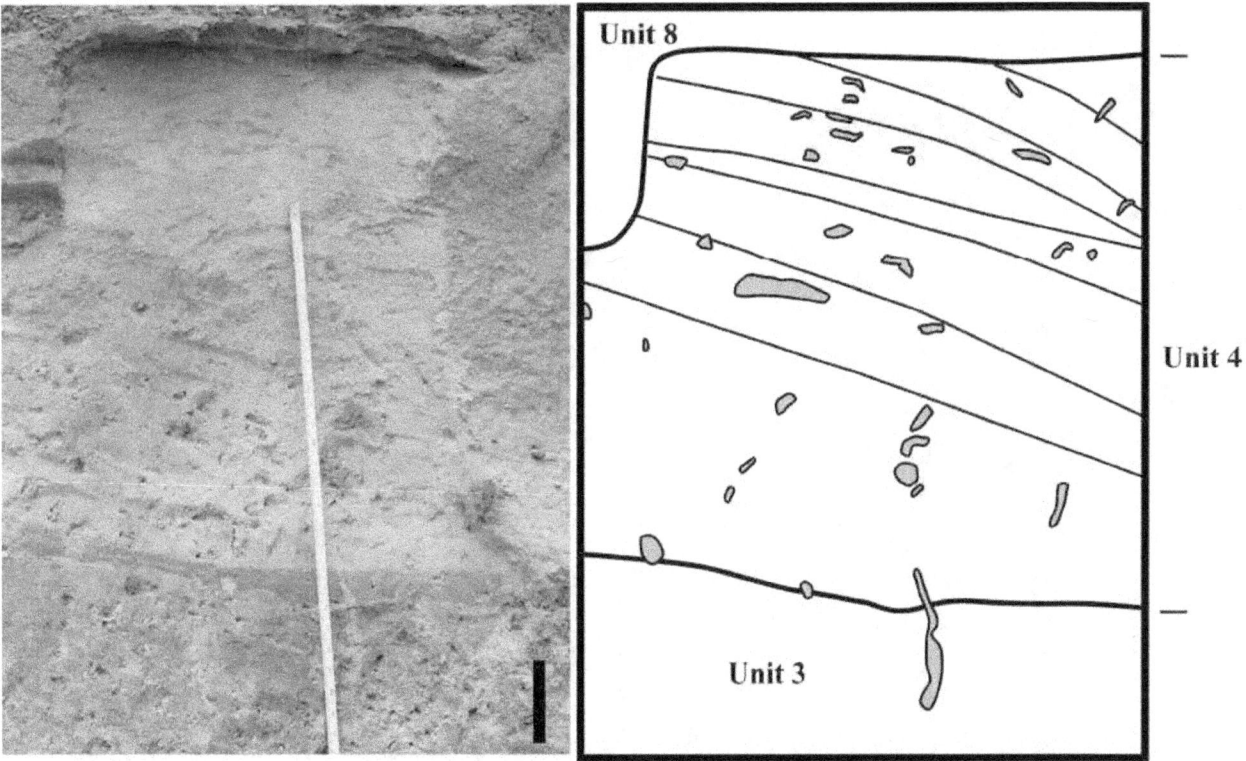

Figure 9. Photograph and sketch of the basal part of unit 4 overlying unit 3 at site 3B. The basal contact of unit 4 is inclined about 10° to the right. The actual unit contact is below the white-red boundary, which is due to a diagenetic mineralization in the porous sand of unit 4 overlying the more impermeable mud of unit 3. Very faint inclined lamination is more readily visible on the weathered surface to the right, although some tool marks reflect changes in grain size. Large cylinders are filled with muddy sediment (brown in photograph) within the sand. Both sand and mud fillings of cylinders (gray in drawing) cut across the contact of the two units. Scale bar is 10 cm long.

In thick occurrences of unit 4, the upper part has orange stains, a clay-rich matrix, more abundant circular and ovate sediment features, and abundant vertical to subhorizontal planar breaks that may be orange stained (figs. 10 and 11). Some of the planar surfaces are small normal faults that offset features by a few centimeters.

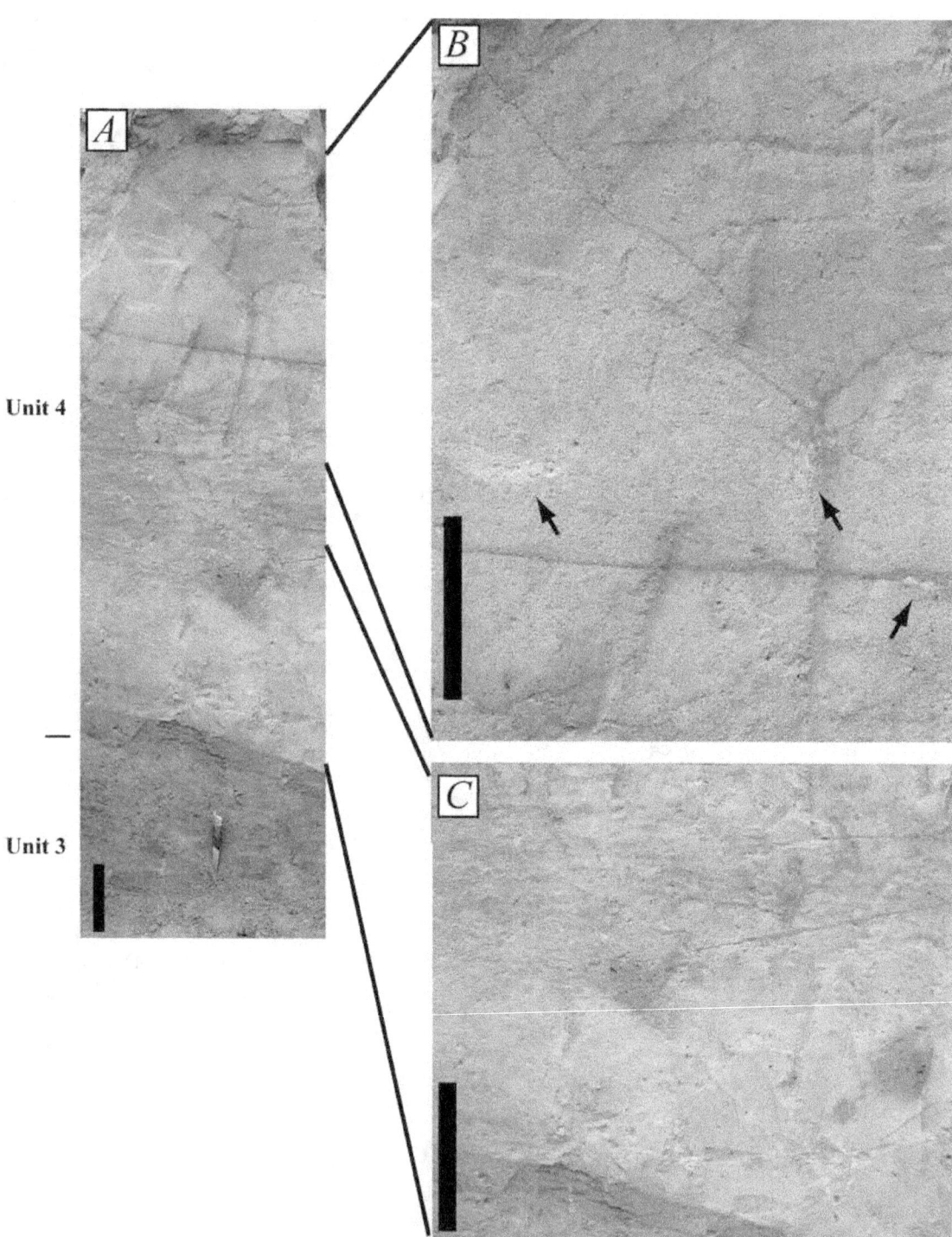

Figure 10. Photographs of exposure at site 4B showing unit 4 overlying unit 3. Note the steeply dipping contact and the iron stain of the lower part of unit 4 as in figure 9. *A*, General view of section showing vertical transition from loose sand at the base to orange-stained muddy sand at the top. Scale bar is 20 cm long. *B*, Detail of upper part of section showing orange-stained horizontal and inclined planar features. White ovate features (arrows) are either injection pipes or bioturbation features. Scale bar is 20 cm long. *C*, Detail of lower part of section showing abundant sediment-filled burrows (gray circular and ovate features). Surrounding sediment is permeated by smaller scale circular and ovate features interpreted as burrows and root casts. Scale bar is 20 cm long.

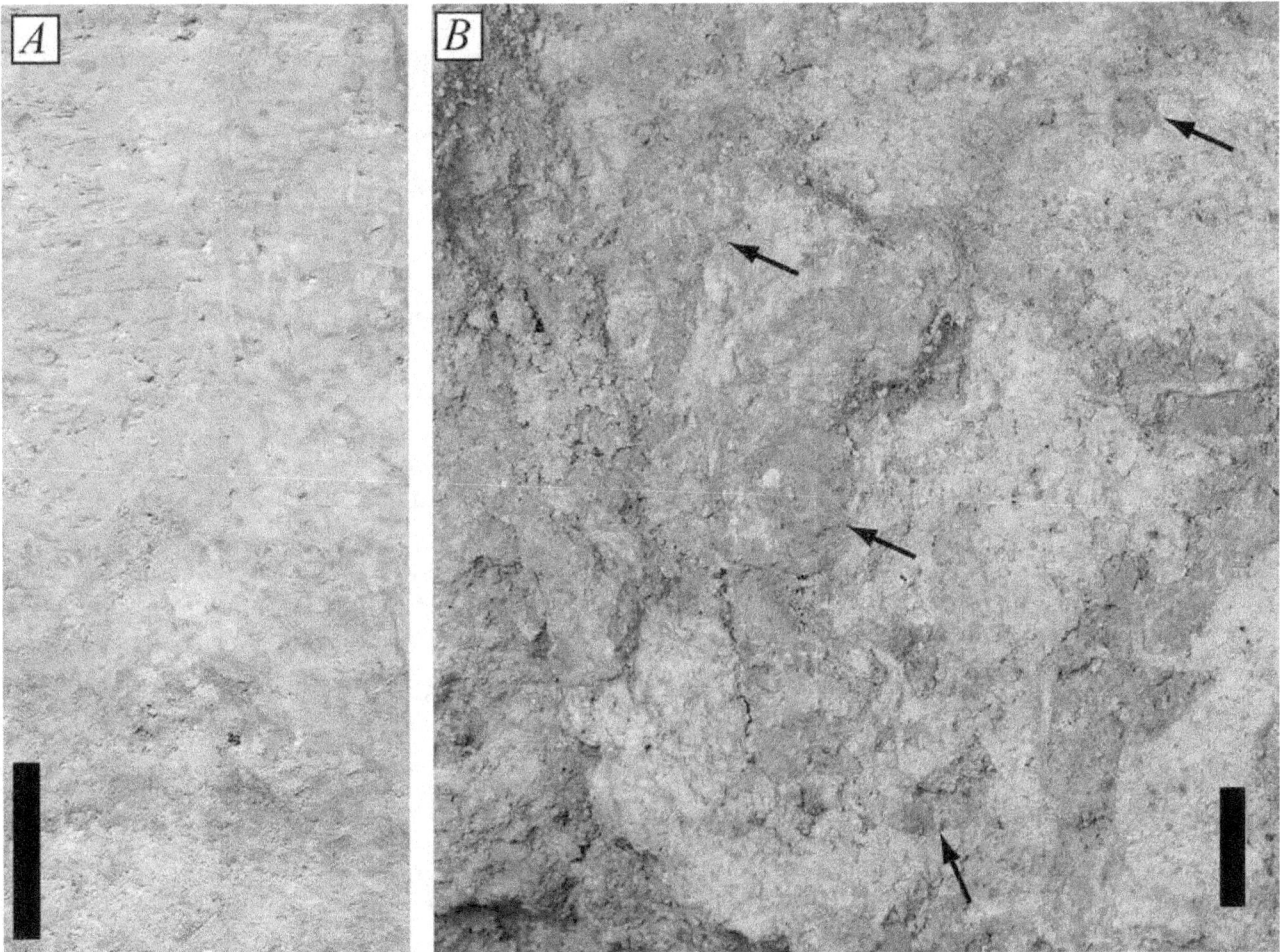

Figure 11. Photographs of the top of unit 4 at site 2B. *A*, Cleaned surface showing transition from loose sand upward to more compact muddy sand. Abundant circular and ovate features of differing color shades are sediment-filled burrows and root casts. Scale bar is 5 cm long. *B*, Broken surface of a hand sample showing a view parallel to bedding. Large mud-filled burrows (black arrows) are crosscut by smaller sand-filled tubes (red arrows) that may be burrows or root casts. Linear features are clay-coated vertical planes interpreted as columnar peds. Note open vesicles (black dots) that include root casts and possible ice crystal casts. Scale bar is 1 cm long.

The grain-size distribution and rounding in unit 4 are consistent with wave sorting. Planar lamination and wavy to lenticular beds with poorly defined internal lamination are both similar to bedding produced by waves (see Bridge and Demicco, 2008, p. 499–507). The dearth of muddy material suggests that wave sorting was continuous as in shallow water along a coastline. The planar inclined contact is interpreted as a wave-cut platform. The transition to unbedded deposits with a clay-rich matrix is interpreted as a soil overprint. Windblown fine-grained material was eluviated into the upper part of the deposit and then deformed by intermittent wetting and drying. This process probably produced the vertical and horizontal planar disruptions. Roots and burrows in the soil environment produced the array of cylindrical cross sections. An additional overprint of deformation features is described in the section below on "Permafrost Structures."

Unit 5

At site 3A, a thin interval of layered sediment (unit 5) overlies unit 4 and is truncated by conglomerates of unit 6. Unit 5 consists of about 20 cm of layered sand and pebble gravel with deformed bedding. Unit 5 gradationally overlies massive sand characteristic of the upper part of unit 4 that contains progressively more irregular pods and lenses of clean, white, granule-sized sand or tightly packed fine gravel all cut by small faults (fig. 12). Unit 5 layering appears to be defined by alternations of orange-stained pebbly sand and white, granule-rich sand. Sand layers appear to be normally graded and to thicken into bowl-shaped deformations. Pebbles that are tightly packed and poorly sorted dominate conglomerate layers.

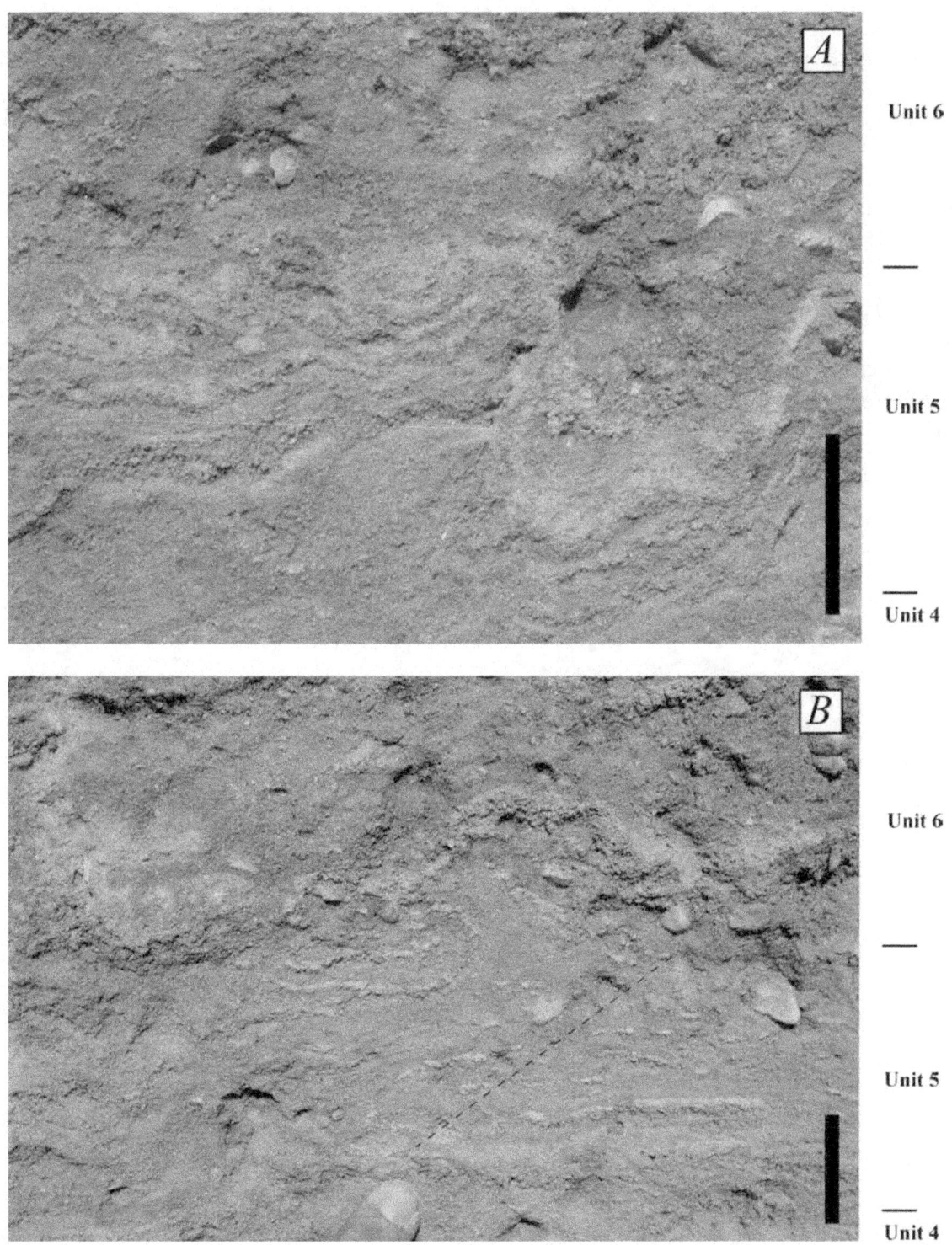

Unit 6

Unit 5

Unit 4

Unit 6

Unit 5

Unit 4

Figure 12. Photographs of irregular bedding in unit 5 between unit 4 and unit 6 at site 3A. *A,* Irregular deformed and podlike layering in sand of unit 5 that is continuous with sand in the underlying unit 4. Note thickening of coarse material into bowl-shaped features and oversteepening of layers. Scale bar is 3 cm long. *B,* Irregular folded bedding and podlike shapes in conglomeratic beds of unit 5 overlying unit 4 and immediately below conglomerate of unit 6. Note segregation of coarse and fine material within lenses. A small fault offsets beds above and to the right of the finger (dashed line). Scale bar is 3 cm long.

The bedding in unit 5 and structures immediately beneath in unit 4 are suggestive of niveo-aeolian deposits as illustrated by Dijkmans (1990) and described by Cailleux (1978), Koster and Dijkmans (1988), and Lewkowicz and Young (1991). In niveo-aeolian deposits, sand is blown onto a snow-covered surface; the snow then melts unevenly over a period of time, deforming the layering, producing small faults, or leaving isolated pods and lenses. Another possible mechanism is freeze-thaw segregation of grain sizes (Van Vliet-Lanoe and others, 1984). These deposits are discussed further in context with other indicators of permafrost conditions; see the section below on "Permafrost Structures."

Unit 6

Unit 6 consists of brownish sand, conglomerate, silt, and clay that are easily cut by a shovel, in contrast to the coarse-grained deposits of unit 2 and unit 3. The unit is defined where it overlies unit 4 or underlies unit 7, but both contacts were not observed at any single locality. At site 4B and continuing southeast for another 30 m, unit 6 deposits occur as lenses containing steeply dipping decimeter-thick beds that tangentially intersect bowl-shaped scour surfaces (figs. 13 and 14).

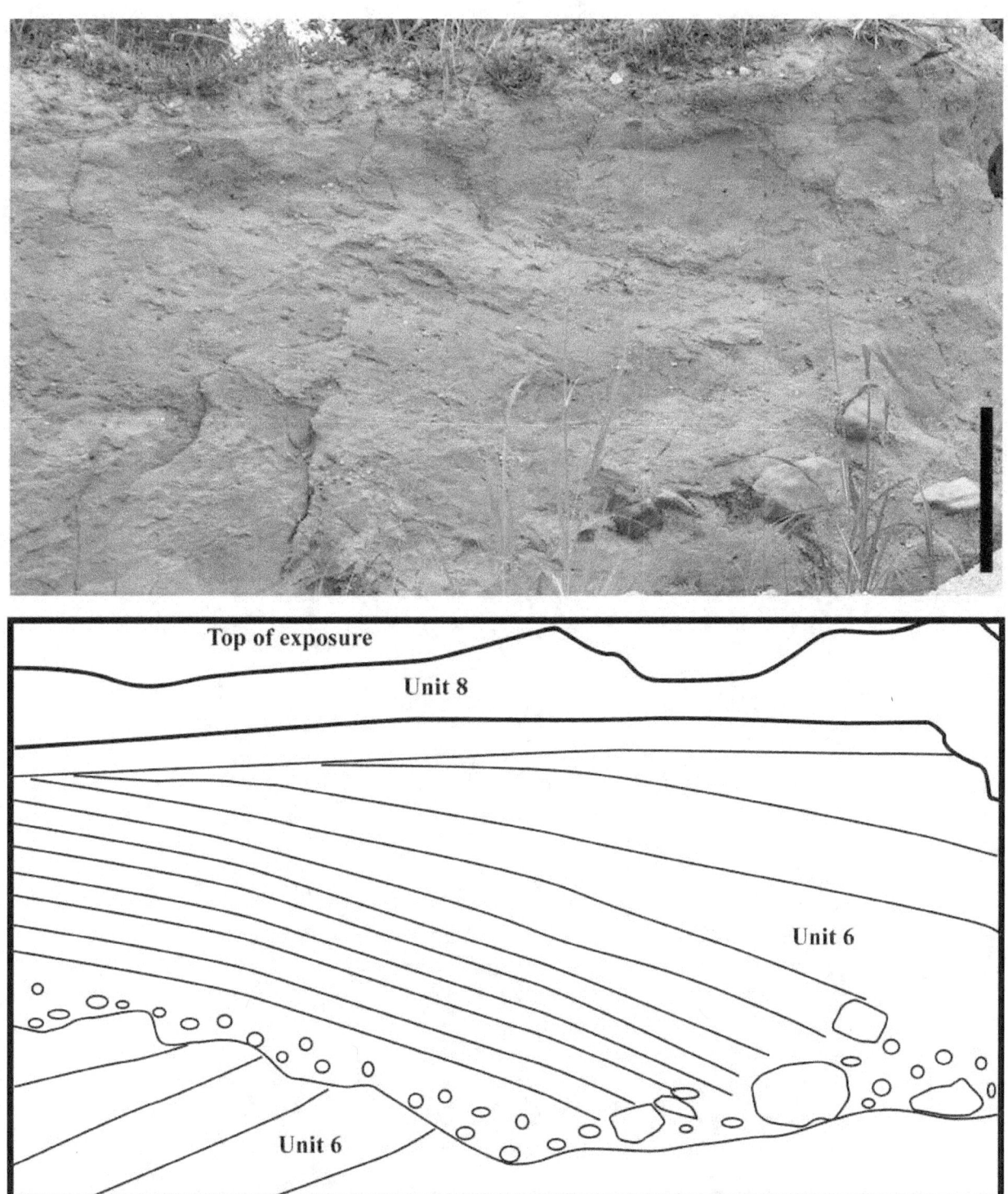

Figure 13. Photograph and sketch of a weathered surface of exposure of unit 6 about 15 m southeast of site 4B. A scour surface dipping to the right has boulders and cobbles along the flat basal contact. Inclined beds parallel to the scour consist of alternations of pebbly sand, fine sand with ripple cross lamination, and thin mud drapes. Ripples indicate flow out of the plane of view (south). Below the scour, similar beds are dipping to the left where they connect with the section shown in figure 14. Scale bar is 50 cm long.

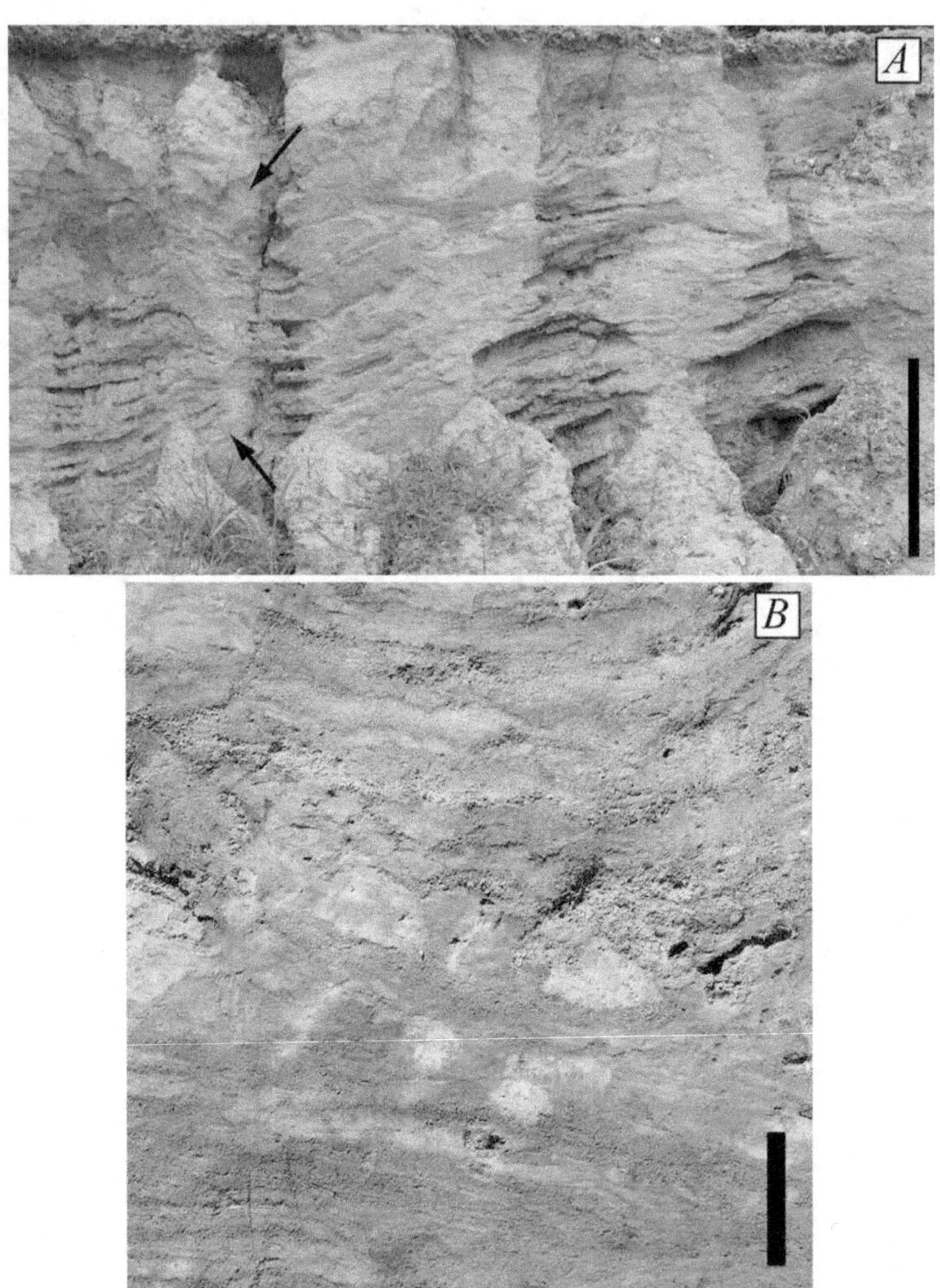

Figure 14. Photographs of unit 6 adjacent to and at site 4B. *A,* Weathered surface of unit 6 in exposure adjacent to site 4B on the left side. Layers standing in relief are mud rich, whereas those that are recessed are pebbly sand. Beds dip to the left and out of the plane of the outcrop. Note changes in bedding dip angles (arrows) indicating internal erosional breaks. Scale bar is 50 cm long. *B,* Detail of cleaned surface of inclined sets of unit 6 at site 4B. Granule-rich sand layers in upper part mark the contact between two inclined bedding sets within unit 6. Light patches are reduction halos associated with sand-filled tubes. Location of the area depicted in this photograph is shown in figure 42. Scale bar is 15 cm long.

Each bed is an alternation of coarse sand or pebbly sand and much finer grained sand or mud. Each bed becomes coarser downdip and finer grained updip. The tangential bases of inclined beds are boulders and cobbles in places, and the upper parts are composed of alternations of fine sand and clay (fig. 15).

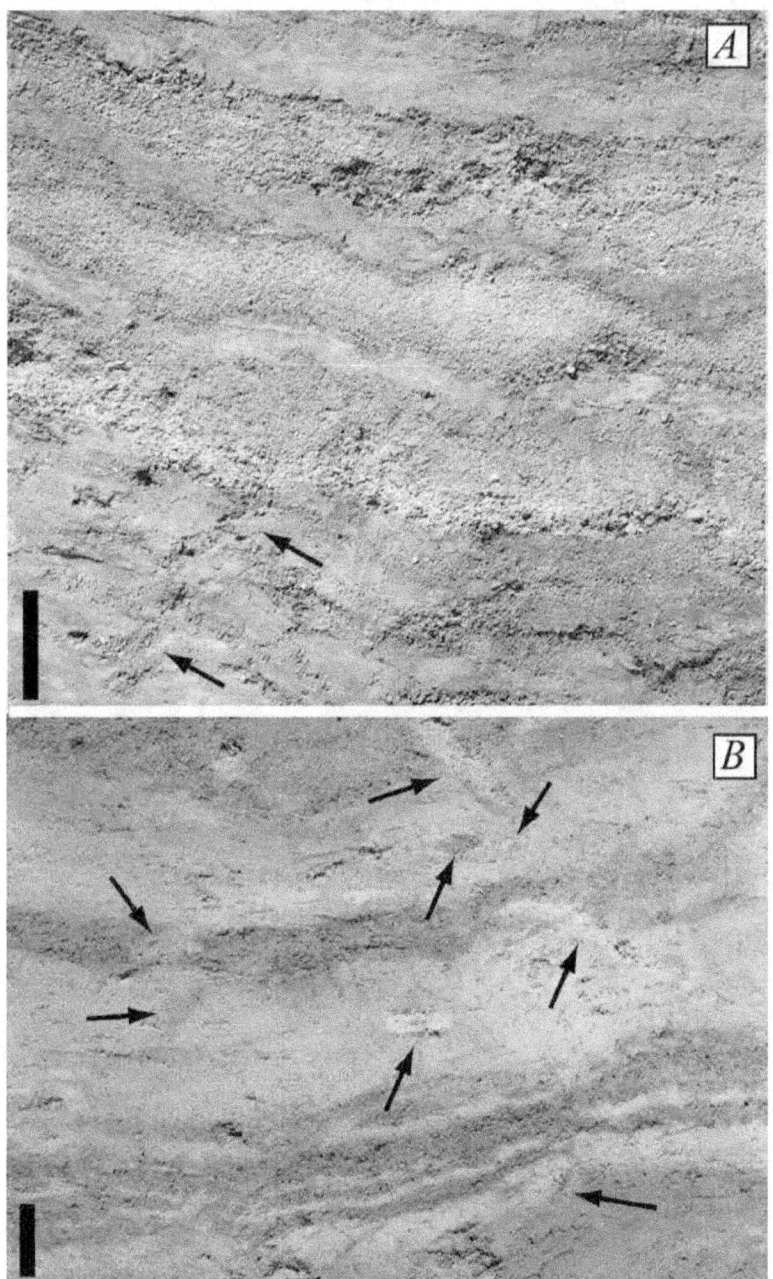

Figure 15. Photographs showing details of sand and mud alternations in inclined sets of unit 6 at site 4B. *A*, Detail of sand and mud alternations in coarse-grained part of inclined sets of unit 6 at site 4B. Note grading of sand and fine gravel and suggestions of inclined bedding (dipping out of exposure). Vertical feature (arrows) is a sand-filled crack interpreted as a desiccation feature. Location of the area depicted in this photograph is shown in figure 42. Scale bar is 4 cm long. *B*, Detail of sand and mud alternations in fine-grained part of inclined sets of unit 6 at site 4B. Circular and ovate features (arrows) are sediment-filled tubes interpreted as burrows. Location of the area depicted in this photograph is shown in figure 42. Scale bar is 2 cm long.

23

Sediment-filled cylindrical features are common within the finer grained portions of the beds of unit 6. The inclinations of the bed sets vary laterally, and two or more orientations may occur in a vertical succession. Some of the sandy portions of beds contain ripple cross lamination. At several different stratigraphic levels and different locations, the geometry of the cross lamination indicates flow to the south and southwest, or at right angles to the direction of bedding inclination. Similar scour fills with inclined bedding were observed along the northeastern wall of the pit.

At site 4A, unit 6 consists of a sand deposit that does not exhibit the inclined sets. At this locality, unit 6 still contains thin mud partings within pebbly sand, and it directly underlies unit 7 (fig. 16). The deposit is composed of sand to pebbly sand as stacks of tabular foresets 20 to 30 cm thick, separated by thin layers of mud. Most of the prominent sets dip to the northwest with subtle indicators of reactivation surfaces. Smaller scale crossbeds appear to dip in the opposite direction.

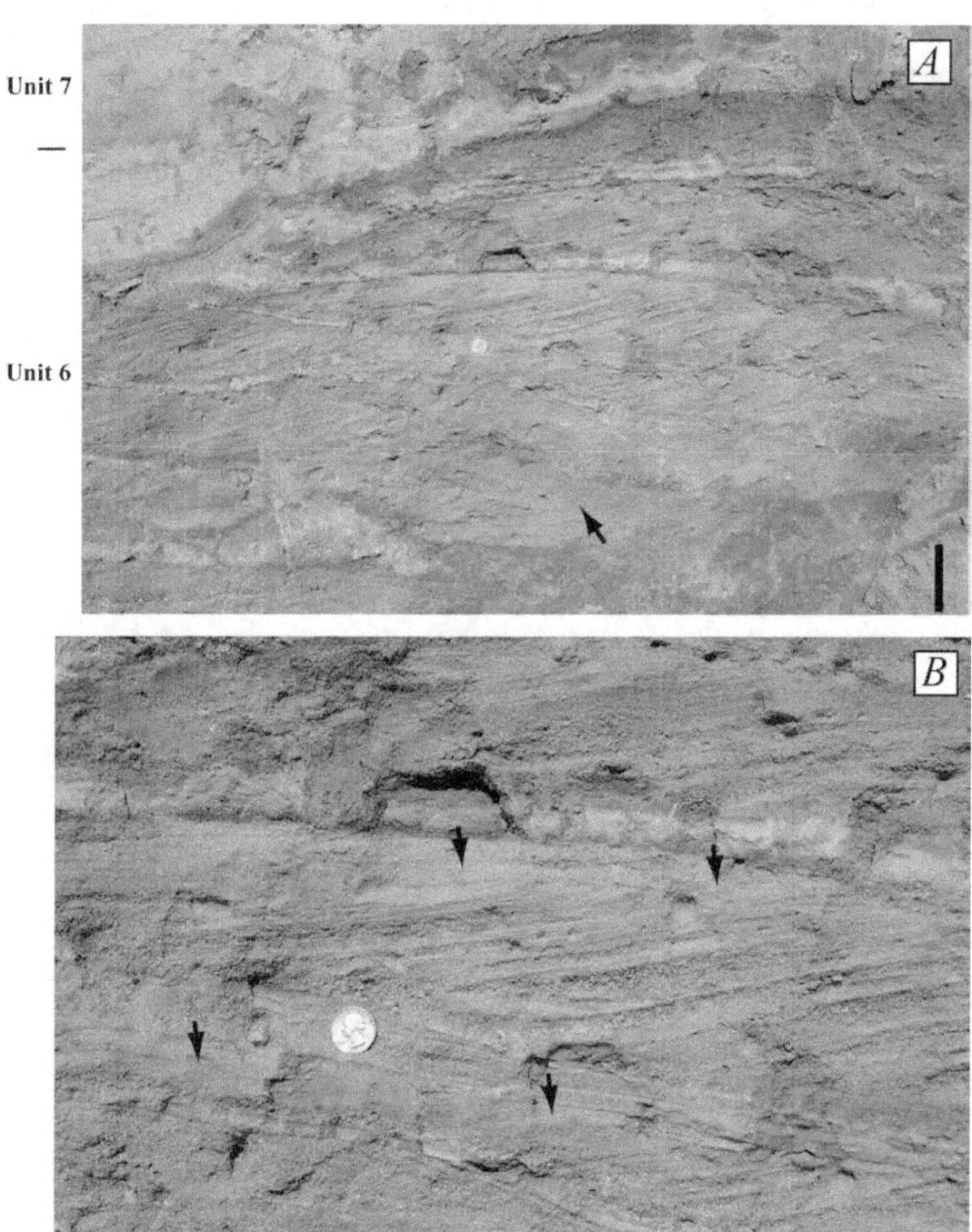

Unit 7

Unit 6

Figure 16. Photographs showing tabular crossbedding in unit 6 at site 4A. *A*, General view of tabular crossbedding with thin mud drapes (light) in unit 6 at site 4A. Crossbeds primarily indicate flow to the left and into the picture (northwest), but a few sets dip to the right (arrow). Light unit in upper left corner is unit 7. Scale bar is 10 cm long. *B*, Detail of crossbedding in area near coin in figure 16*A*. Note reactivation surfaces (arrows) and cross lamination dipping to the right at the center base of the picture. Coin is 2.5 cm in diameter.

At site 1A, there is a thin interval of sand alternating with pebble conglomerate (including a mud-clast conglomerate) that is overlain by mottled pebbly sand (fig. 17), capped by silt of unit 7. This is assigned to unit 6, but it could also be part of unit 2 and unit 3. The complete segregation of sand and pebble conglomerate into decimeter-thick beds and the presence of mud intraclasts suggest an affinity to unit 6 at sites 4A and 4B. The thick mottled interval, however, is more like unit 3 than like unit 6 observed elsewhere.

At site 5B, a boulder conglomerate overlain by crossbeds of pebble conglomerate and sand also has thin mud partings and is assigned to unit 6 (fig. 18). Laterally, the unit consists of alternations of sand and mud similar to those at site 4B. This deposit directly overlies unit 2 and has no overlying deposit.

Muddy layers in all occurrences of unit 6 appear to be cut by scattered sand-filled cylinders. The basal contact of the unit varies over 2 to 3 m in elevation; in places, the contact steeply truncates units 3 and 4, and, at site 5B, it directly overlies unit 2.

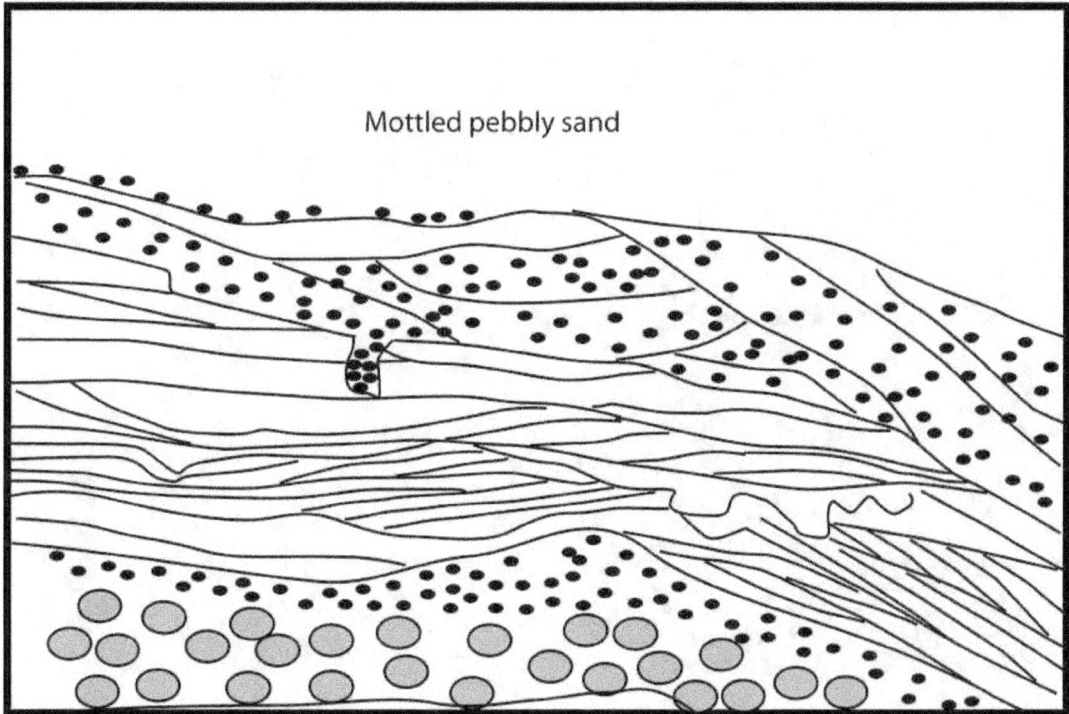

Mottled pebbly sand

Figure 17. Photograph and sketch of interbedded pebble conglomerate and crossbedded sand of unit 6 at site 1A. Conglomerate at the base of the exposure contains numerous mud intraclasts (gray in drawing). Crossbedding consists of compound tabular foresets that are dipping out of the picture (south). Note the deformation features (arrows) that may be due to ice melting. Upper part of exposure is a mottled pebbly sand. Scale bar is 20 cm long.

Figure 18. Photographs of weathered exposures of unit 6 at site 5B and about 20 m southeast of site 5B. *A*, Weathered exposure at site 5B where boulder and cobble conglomerate of unit 6 overlies compact pebbly sand assigned to unit 2. Upper pebble conglomerate and sand alternations are trough crossbeds dipping into the plane of the picture (southwest). The bed sets are separated by sandy mud layers (arrows). Scale bar is 20 cm long. *B*, Weathered exposure of sand and mud alternations in unit 6 about 20 m southeast of site 5B. Note cross lamination in the fine sand layer (arrow) indicating flow out of the picture (northeast). Scale bar is 10 cm long.

The rhythmic alternation of coarse-grained sediment with mud drapes that characterizes unit 6 (figs. 13–18) is interpreted as evidence of tidal influence in sedimentation (see for instance, Weimer and others, 1982). Coarse-grained sediment is deposited during flood tide or ebb tide flow, whereas mud drapes are deposited during slack water conditions of full tide. The tidal influence on this unit is supported by the bimodal orientation of crossbedding at site 4A. The inclined sets at site 4B are interpreted as lateral-accretion sets of high-sinuosity meandering tidal channels (see Weimer and others, 1982, fig. 5). The area composed of tabular foresets resembles a tidal-bar deposit with the coarse-grained sediment alternating with mud drapes. The coarseness of grain size in these deposits is not typical of most tidal deposits. The similarity of provenance for unit 6 and unit 2 is interpreted as evidence of localized reworking of the older deposits.

Unit 7

Unit 7 shows a great deal of variability in sedimentary character over the area of the pit. Each section cleaned produced a different succession of textures, and the lateral relationships were not established. At site 1B along the southwestern wall, tan silt with scattered sand and small pebbles dominates a unit about 70 cm thick (fig. 19). The basal contact is flat, overlying pebbly sand and conglomerate of either unit 2 or unit 3 and is defined by a line of well-rounded pebbles having long axes 1 to 3 cm long (fig. 20).

Above the contact at site 1B, the lowest 15 cm of unit 7 is rich in gray mud and well-sorted sand suggesting centimeter-scale thin beds but heavily disrupted by sediment-filled cylinders. Silt dominates for the rest of the thickness and has evidence for abundant sediment-filled cylinders of varying diameters and narrow vertical cracks spaced about 60 to 80 cm apart (fig. 19). Cylinders of carbon about 4 cm in diameter are oriented horizontally and restricted to the upper 10 to 15 cm of this exposure. The cylinders are filled with layered sand at the base and laminated silt at the top. The sediment becomes dark gray near the upper contact.

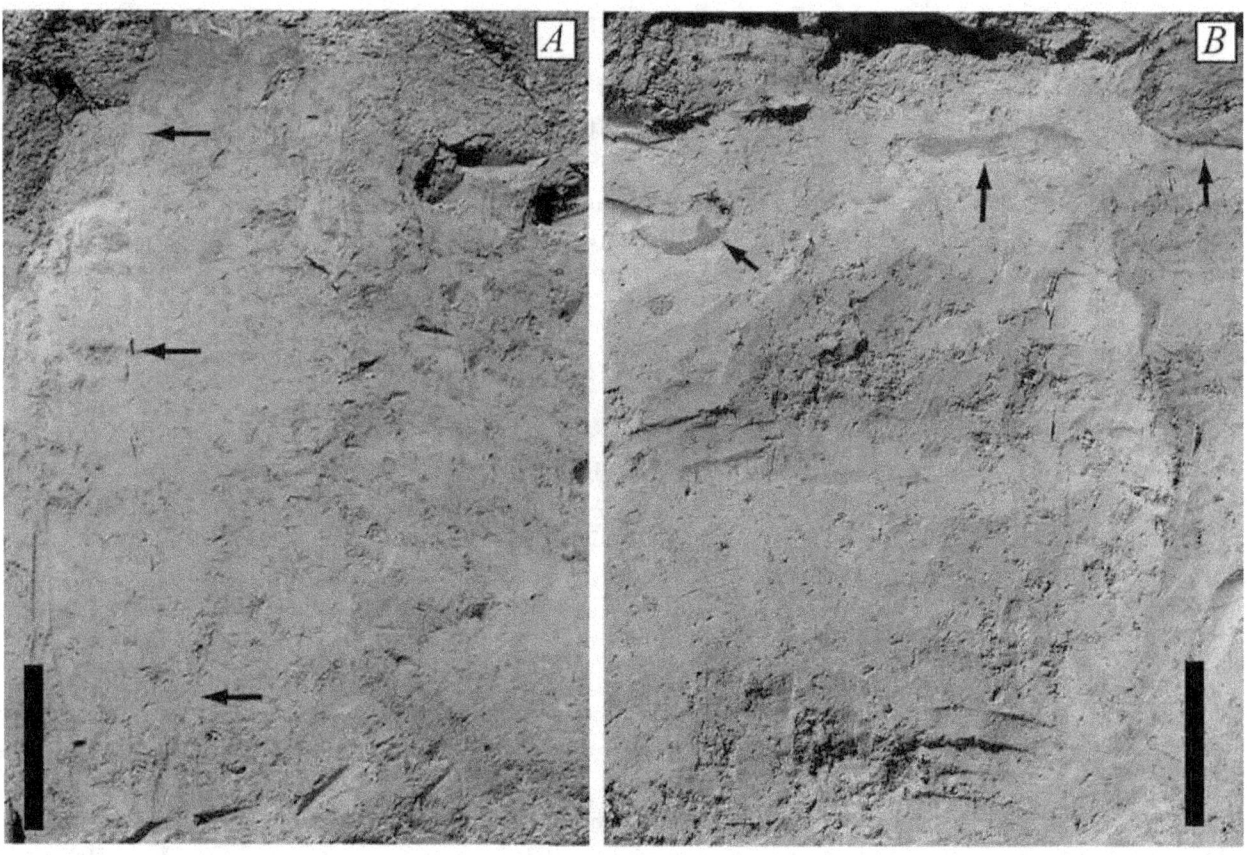

Figure 19. Photographs of unit 7 at site 1B. *A*, General view of unit 7 at site 1B. Base is interbedded sand and mud (pale gray), whereas the rest of the section is tan silt with scattered pebbles. Dark-gray cap of sequence is interpreted as a soil A horizon. Vertical feature (arrows) is a planar crack interpreted as a columnar soil ped. Scale bar is 30 cm long. *B*, Detail of upper part of unit 7 at site 1B. Mottled texture of tan silt is due to abundant sediment-filled tubes interpreted as burrows and root casts. Dark irregularities on surface are pits where scattered pebbles were plucked free by cleaning. Large root casts (arrows) have a geopetal fill of laminated sediment draping an irregular mud base and a carbon rim. These roots are oriented parallel to the bedding surface. Scale bar is 10 cm long.

Silt

Mottled
sand and
mud

Unit 2?

Figure 20. Photograph showing basal part of unit 7 overlying unit 2(?) at site 1B. Unit 7 contact with unit 2(?) is marked by a line of pebbles (arrows). Lower 15 cm is mostly sand with irregular clumps of mud (gray) and silt. Circular to ovate mottled texture is due to abundant sediment-filled burrows. Upper part of picture shows tan silt that also has circular to ovate mottles due to bioturbation. Scale bar is 10 cm long.

A few meters away from site 1B on the northwestern wall of the pit, the silt unit is about 1.5 m thick and directly overlies orange pebble conglomerate. In this exposure, the silt has multiple bands of coarser and finer silt, each about 1 cm thick (fig. 21). The layering appears to cease laterally against a deformed contact with sediment similar to the underlying unit.

Figure 21. Photographs of unit 7 on northwest wall immediately adjacent to site 1B. *A*, General view showing centimeter-scale lamination grading upward to mottled textures. White circular features and linear features are filled with sand. Vertical features (arrows) are planar cracks mostly filled with muddy silt. Scale bar is 20 cm long. *B*, Detail of layering shown in figure 21*A*. Lighter bands are siltier and dark bands are muddier. Sand-filled features are tube shaped. Long vertical feature on left side of photograph roughly follows a vertical crack mostly filled with muddy silt. Scale bar is 5 cm long.

At site 2B, unit 7 directly overlies heavily mottled sand of unit 4 (fig. 22). At this locality, there appear to be two thick silt beds separated by 20 cm of an orangish fine sand layer. The basal contact of the fine sand layer is sharp and planar on the underlying silt, but the upper contact is gradational and mottled. The uppermost part of unit 7 is muddier, grayer, and more similar to the exposure at site 1B. All silt and sand beds are disrupted by numerous sediment-filled tubes and some open tubes (fig. 23). Finer grained silt layers have a pattern of horizontal vesicles that are less than 0.5 mm in cross section (fig. 24). Cylindrical vugs that are elongate on the horizontal plane are commonly associated with these narrow vesicles. The sand layers also have open vugs that are circular in cross section and tubular in plan view and vertical sections. These commonly have thin walls of dense material that is orange or yellow. Smear slides of the silt and fine sand from site 2B indicate that the grains are very angular and poorly sorted. Clay-sized grains appear to consist mostly of quartz or feldspar rather than clay minerals. Sand-sized grains in the sand and silt layers have a frosted sheen suggestive of aeolian polishing. At site 4A, there appear to be as many as four gray silt beds separated by orange fine sand (see figure 38).

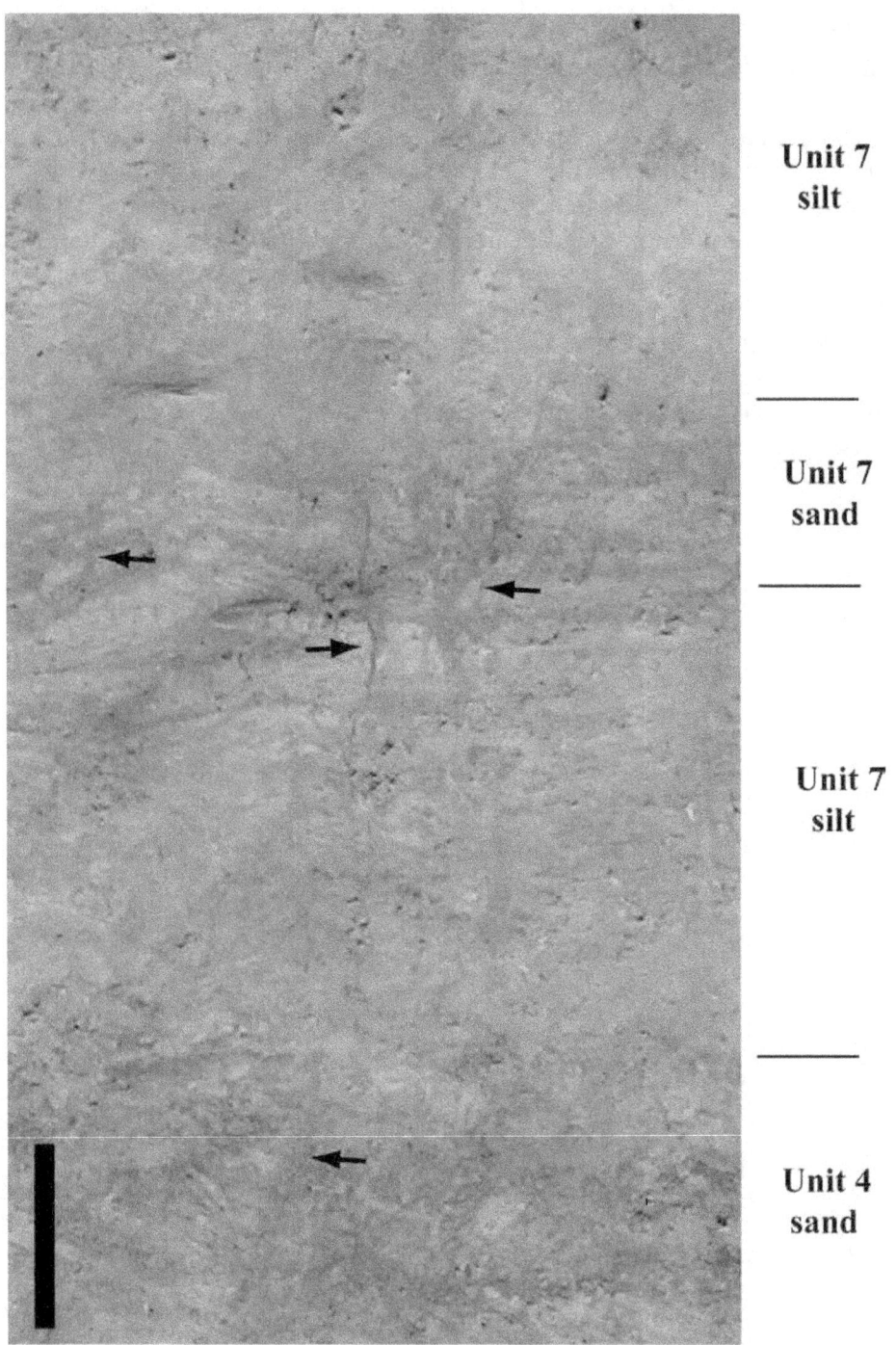

Unit 7
silt

Unit 7
sand

Unit 7
silt

Unit 4
sand

Figure 22. Photograph of exposure at site 2B showing contact between unit 7 (above) and unit 4. Grayish silt of unit 7 overlies mottled sand of unit 4. Upper part of unit 7 is a tan silt that is dark gray towards the top. A thin, orange-stained sand with abundant silt clumps sharply caps the lower silt. Vertical structures (arrows) are sediment-filled wedges. Mottled circular to ovate pattern throughout section is due to burrows and root casts. Scale bar is 20 cm long.

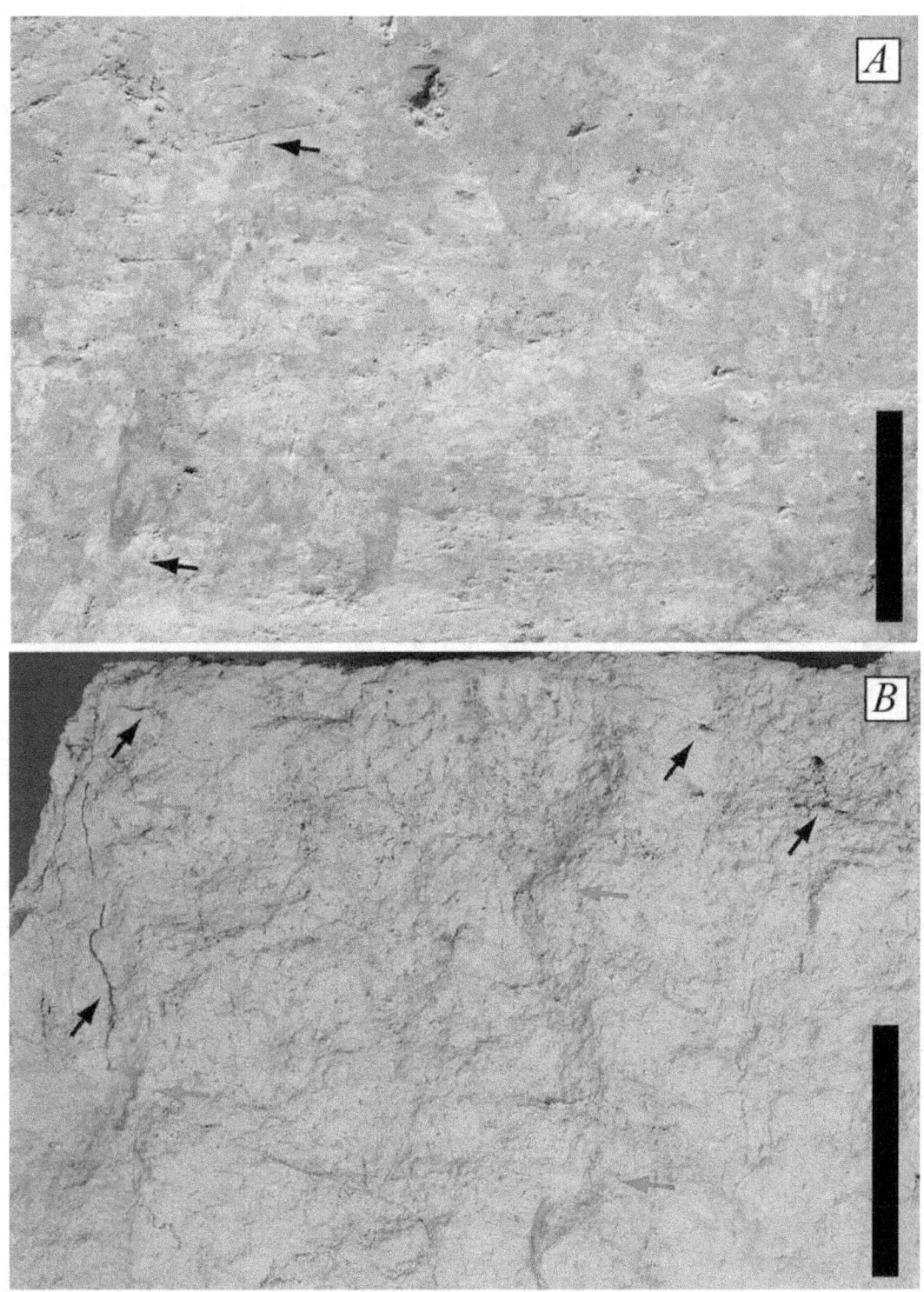

Figure 23. Photographs showing details of sedimentary fabrics of unit 7 at site 2B. *A*, Typical fabric of the lower silt layer just below contact with sand in unit 7. Circular and ovate features are mostly sediment-filled burrows. A sediment-filled wedge (arrows) indicates that the wedge filling was subsequently disrupted by burrows. Scale bar is 10 cm long. *B*, Typical fabric at top of unit 7. Burrow features are less distinct, and carbon-filled root casts (black arrows) or open root casts (brownish spots) are common. Planar vertical parting features (red arrows) are interpreted as columnar peds. Scale bar is 10 cm long.

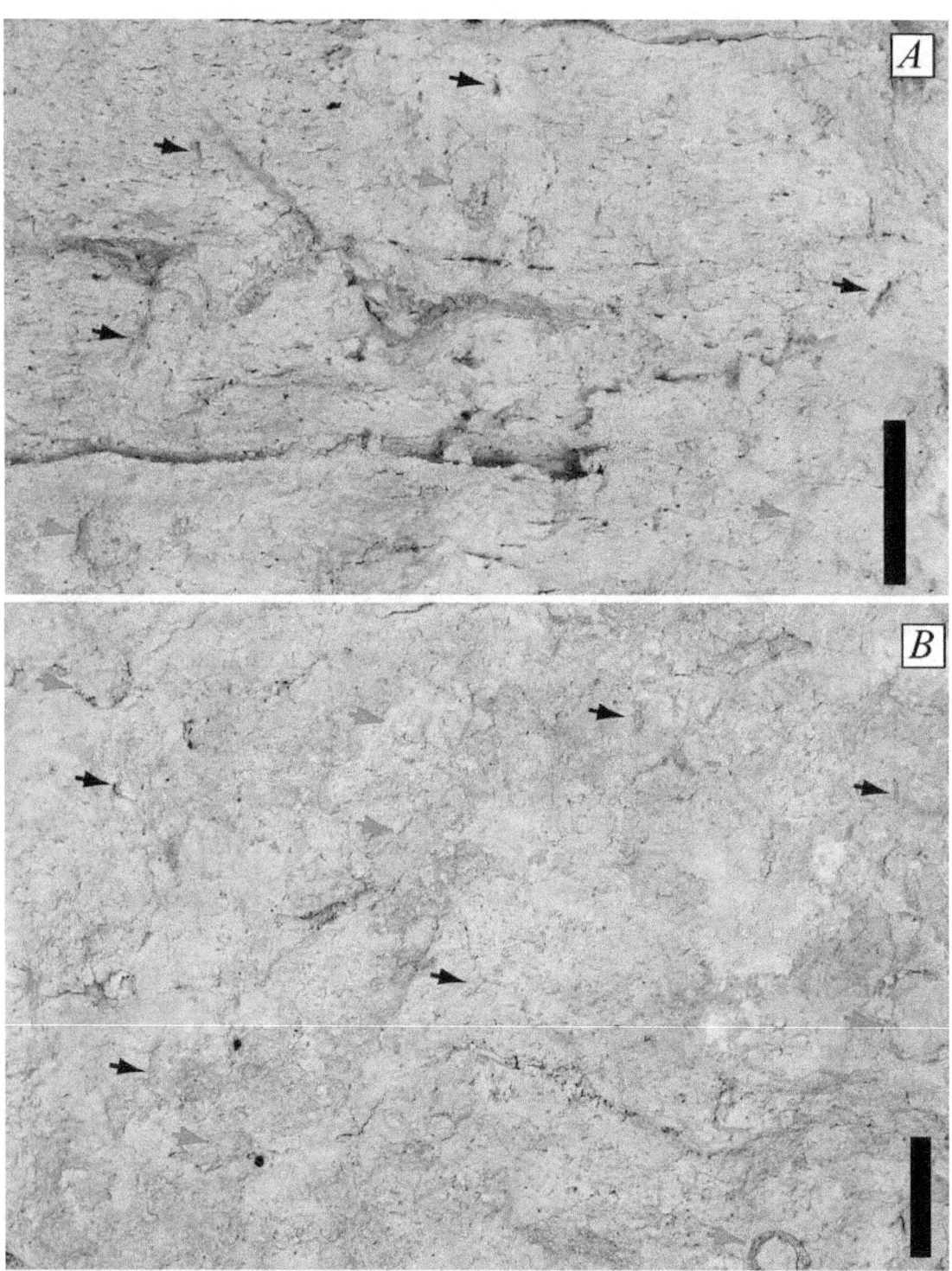

Figure 24. Photographs of hand samples of lower silt layer in unit 7 at site 2B. *A,* Cross section of silt showing flattened vesicles (small dark dashes). Silt is disturbed by root casts (black arrows) and sediment-filled burrows (red arrows). Note curved layering in sediment filling of burrow (spreiten) in the left central part of photograph. Scale bar is 1 cm long. *B,* Plan view section of silt at contact with sand. Large sediment-filled tubes (red arrows) are vertical (circular cross sections) and horizontal (elongate). Root casts (black arrows) are mostly horizontal. Sand bed is partly visible at bottom of photograph showing open vugs (black specks). Scale bar is 2 cm long.

If the site 2B samples are reflective of the entire unit, the mud devoid of clay minerals and the highly angular silt and fine sand both suggest deposition as loess derived from a glacial deposit. Wah (2003) interpreted the sheet of silt covering the Delmarva highlands as loess, based on the sorting, non-erosive contact, and apparent age. At least intermittent aeolian transport is suggested by the frosted surfaces of the coarser sand grains in unit 7. The original environment of deposition for most of unit 7 is difficult to determine because of extensive bioturbation indicated by the sediment-filled cylindrical features. Some of the bioturbation is within a soil profile superimposed on the deposit, as indicated by the upward increase of mud (including clay minerals), the carbon-filled root casts, and the narrow planar vertical features suggestive of columnar soil structures. The persistence of bioturbation features indicating both burrows and roots throughout the deposit, however, indicates that the depositional environment also supported this activity. The pattern of fine vesicles in the silt layers is similar to features produced in wet flats covered with algal mats (see Demicco and Hardie, 1994, p. 64–65), although there are also similarities to the microlenticular cryostructure formed by small ice crystals (Bray and others, 2006, fig. 4c). The tubes associated with the vesicular structure, however, reflect bioturbation by animals and root disruption. Roots tending to parallel the surface are common in wet, marshy settings that would also produce the algal mats. Some of the vertical wedge-shaped features may also be indicative of desiccation cracks, although some are clearly cryogenic (see section below on "Permafrost Structures"). Sandy interbeds are thoroughly mixed with the silt but have a sharp basal contact. The lack of internal structure in the sand layers precludes identification of the depositional conditions, although the frosted character of grains also suggests aeolian transport.

Unit 8

Unit 8 consists of brown, compact muddy sand and conglomerate that compose irregular beds about 10 to 30 cm thick at the top of the pit (fig. 25). These beds are very poorly sorted and commonly contain bits of glass and plastic. Open casts of roots and sediment-filled burrows are common. In several places, particularly on the southwestern end of the pit, coarse conglomerates steeply truncate unit 1 (fig. 26). These conglomerates are less consolidated than unit 2 and commonly contain large clasts of unit 1 and fragments of platy iron oxide.

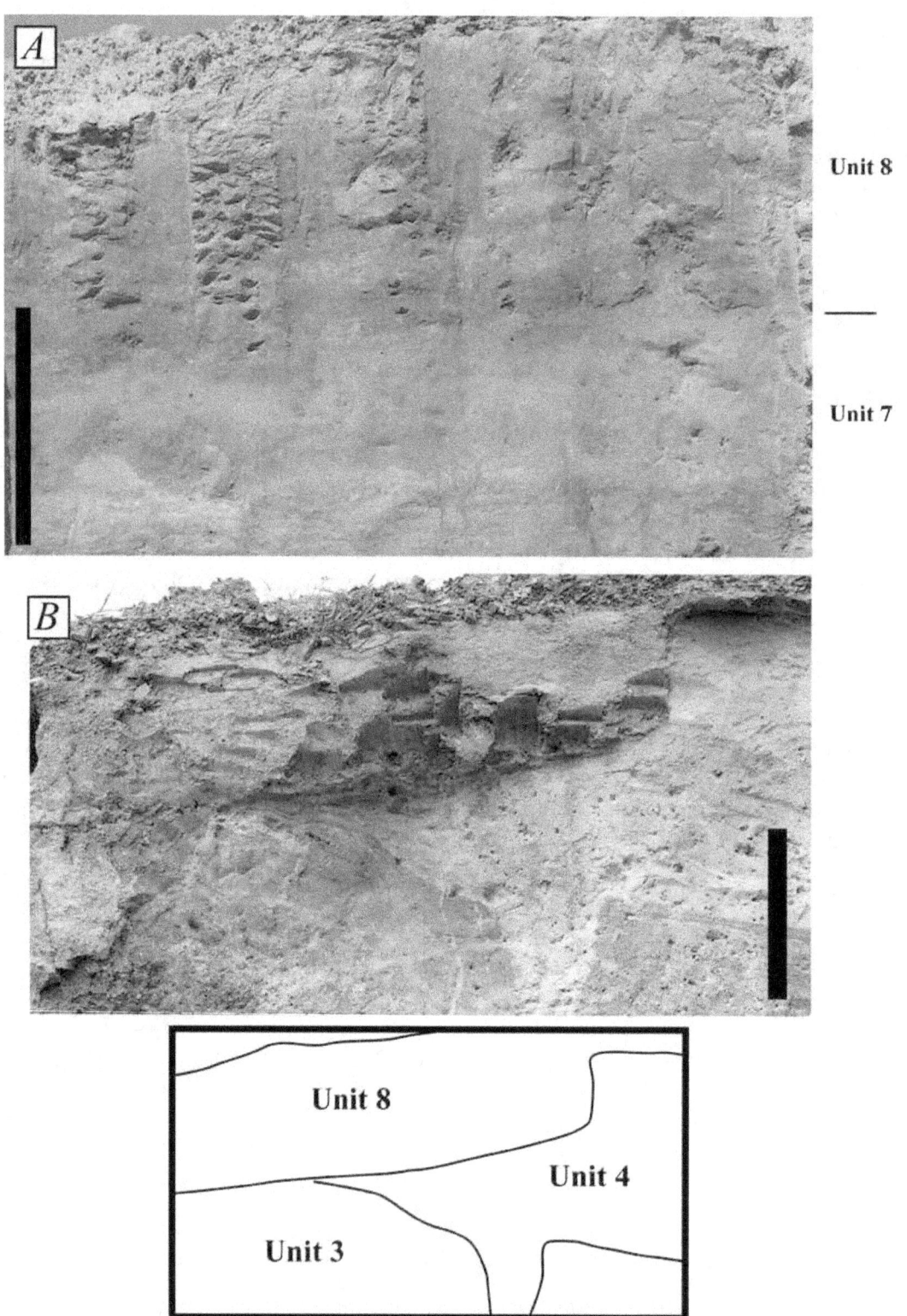

Figure 25. Photograph of unit 8 contact overlying unit 7 at site 2B and photograph and sketch of unit 8 overlying units 3 and 4 at site 3B. *A*, Thick layered sequence of unit 8 overlying unit 7 at site 2B. The layers are composed of muddy sand and are gently inclined to the left and into the pit. Pieces of glass and plastic were found in these beds. Scale bar is 50 cm long. *B*, Lens-shaped muddy conglomerate of unit 8 overlying units 3 and 4 at site 3B. Clasts within this muddy conglomerate include the bluish diabase used on the road. Scale bar is 30 cm long.

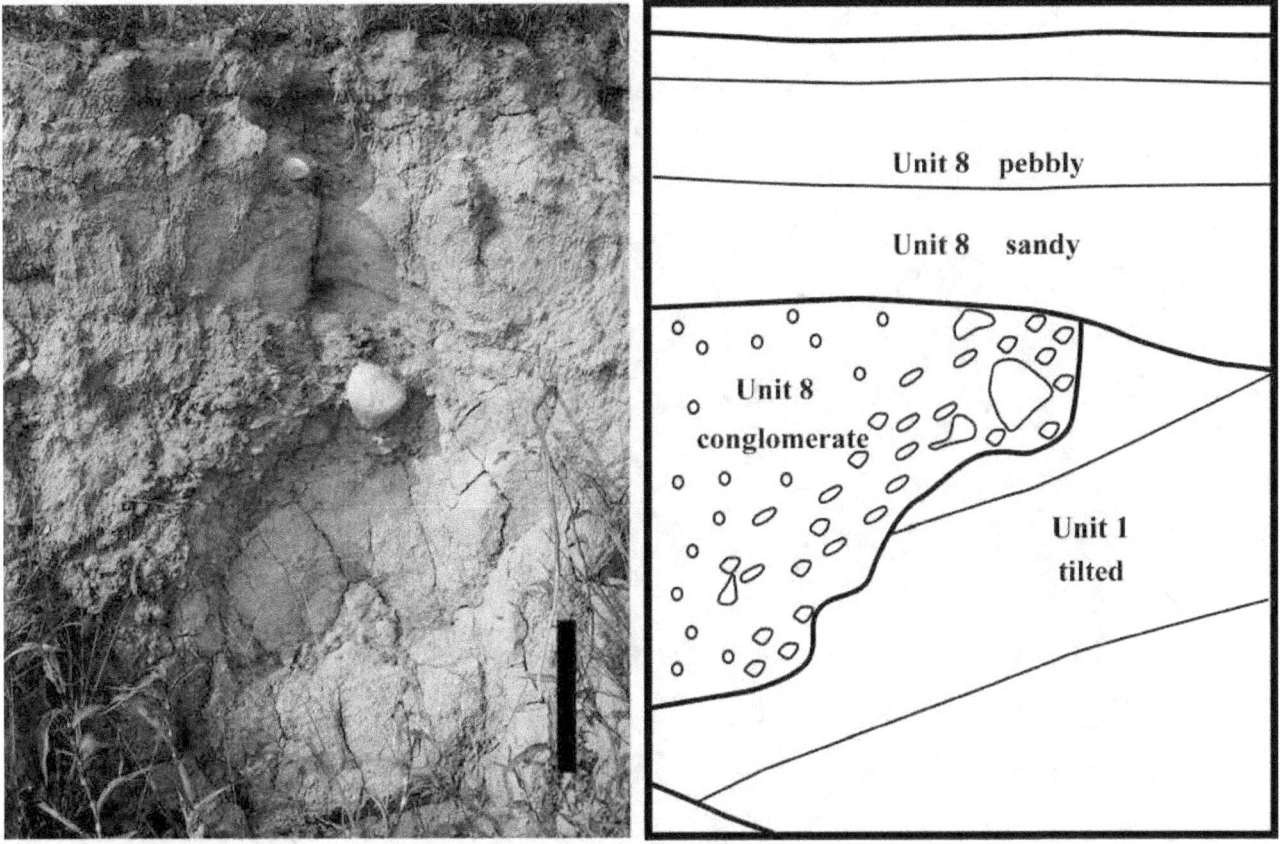

Figure 26. Photograph and sketch of muddy conglomerate in unit 8 filling a steep scour into unit 1 near site 5B. Conglomerate includes large clasts of unit 1 and platy fragments of iron oxide probably derived from the base of unit 2. Unit 1 beds are tilted to the left and into the pit. The basal contact of the muddy sand overlying conglomerate is also inclined toward the pit (toward viewer) and contains numerous roots and open burrows. The inclined bedding is interpreted as wall slump into the pit. Scale bar is 30 cm long.

Unit 8 is interpreted as artificial fill produced from road building and excavation of the pit. Some of this fill probably predates the opening of the Midshore Regional Solid Waste Facility and may have had a soil profile developed. At site 6B, the roadbed was built up a couple of meters, producing beds inclined toward the pit center. The open-framework boulder-cobble beds are believed to be artificial fill that has been modified by running water along rills cut into the pit walls.

Permafrost Structures

French and others (2003, 2005, 2007) described a variety of features that they attributed to Pleistocene permafrost and thermokarst in the coastal plain deposits of New Jersey. During fieldwork for the Volunteer for Science Program of the U.S. Geological Survey, H.M. French and M. Demitroff (written commun., 2007) observed similar features in the coastal plain of Delaware and Maryland. The primary features they observed were wedge-shaped, vertical, sediment-filled structures cutting through sand and gravel deposits, which they interpreted as cryogenic sand wedges and ice wedges, and an assemblage of faults, folds, and vertical-edged pockets of sediment, which they interpreted as features produced by the thawing of permafrost (thermokarst). Most of the deposits in New Jersey were fluvial or aeolian, and aeolian sand was an important component of wedge filling and deformed bedding.

At the Midshore Regional Solid Waste Facility study site, vertical, sediment-filled, wedge-shaped features were observed cutting units 3, 4, 5, and 7. Wedge-shaped features that are almost certainly cryogenic, following the criteria of French (2008), are generally 50 cm to a meter long, have a wide upper portion that contains chevron fillings of the overlying beds, and penetrate both sand and conglomerate (figs. 27 and 28).

Figure 27. Photograph of wedge-shaped structure at contact between units 5 and 6 (arrows) at site 3A. Note progressive inclination of sand and pebble layers into the wide upper part of the wedge and inclination of pebbles to parallel the wedge wall. The wedge extends downward into sand of unit 4. These features are consistent with an ice wedge. Scale bar is 5 cm long.

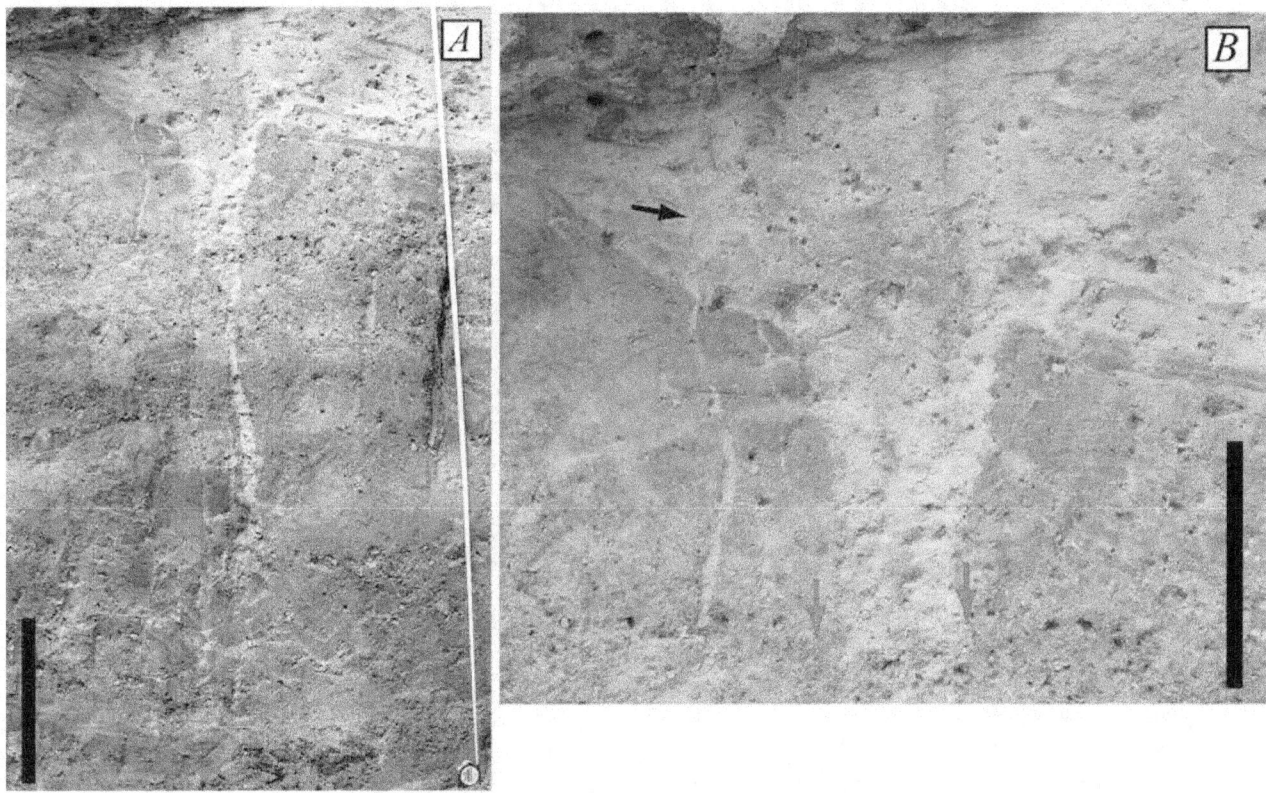

Figure 28. Photographs of wedge-shaped structures in units 3 and 4 at site 3B. *A*, Sand- and pebble-filled wedge extends about 1.5 m through unit 4 sand and interbedded pebbly sand and sandy mud of unit 3. Scale bar is 40 cm long. *B*, Detail of upper part of wedges showing V-shaped filling of upper part of large wedge and smaller wedge to the left (black arrow). Note downward bend of upper surface of pebble layer into the wedge (red arrow). Scale bar is 20 cm long.

Some features in unit 7 have less distinct filling sequences but are continuous with features that cut through sand layers below (fig. 29). At site 2B, the wedge-shaped features are overprinted by abundant burrow and root structures. At site 4B, wedge-shaped features in unit 6 cut only a few beds and are mostly filled by a single layer of overlying sediment (fig. 15*A*). Wedge-shaped features with only local sediment fill and short penetration are also found in unit 7 (figs. 21*A* and 22). These features may be desiccation cracks. If so, they may also have been subsequently modified by sand injected upward from unit 4 (see discussion below).

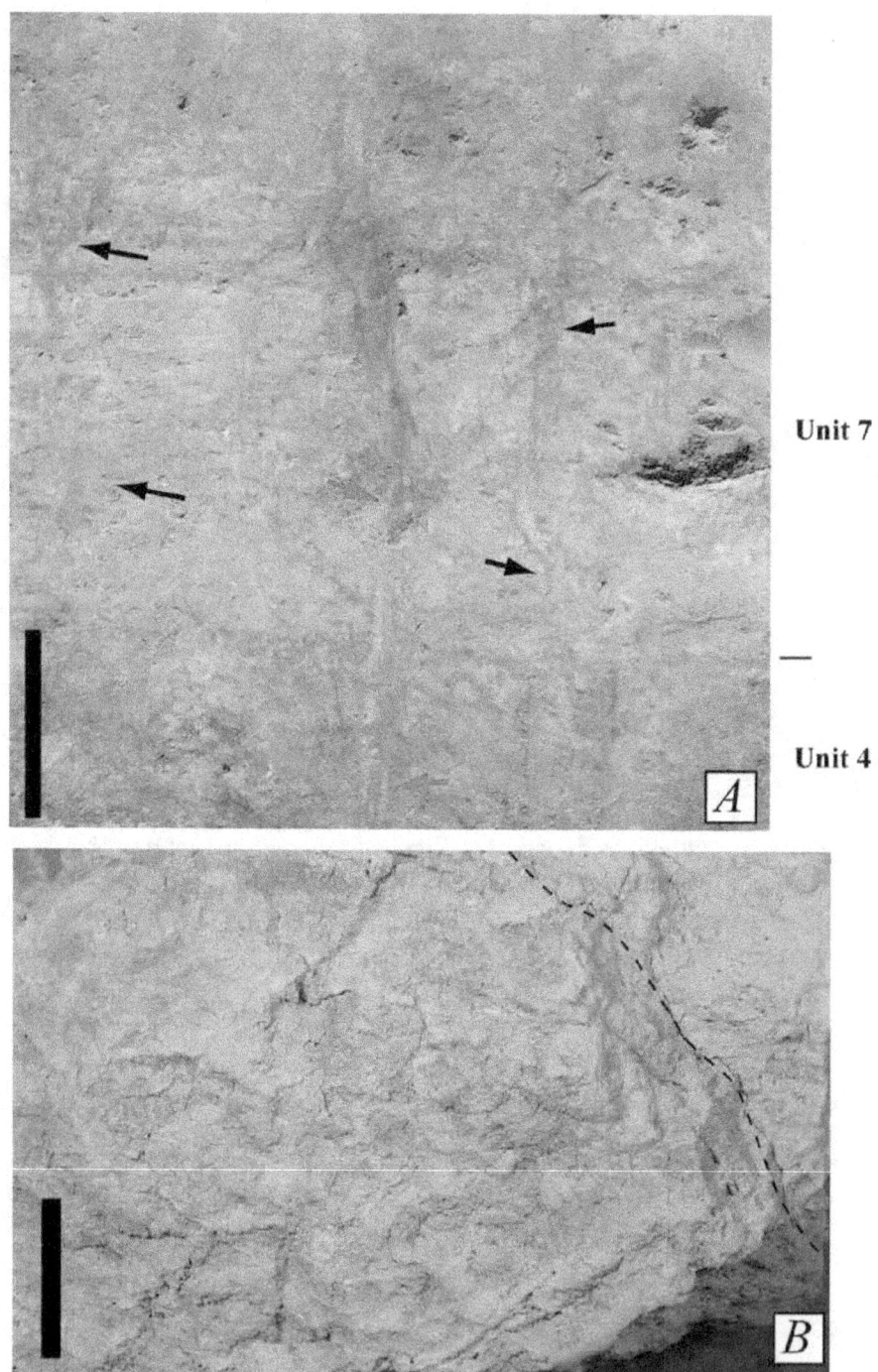

Figure 29. Photographs of wedge-shaped structures in units 7 and 4 at site 2B. *A*, General view of section showing a 1.5-m-long wedge (red arrows) extending through unit 7 and into sand of unit 4. Multiple V-shaped fillings of different sediment are visible along the length. Smaller wedge-shaped features (black arrows) have simpler fillings and do not appear to extend into unit 4. Lower part of wedge on right appears to connect to a sand-filled cylinder extending upward from lower unit 4. Note how wedges fade toward upper part of section. This fading is due to an overprint of bioturbation and soil features from the upper contact. Scale bar is 40 cm long. *B*, Hand sample of unit 7 showing oblique contact between a vertical wedge (left of dashed line) and the surrounding silt. Note that the wedge filling contains abundant circular and ovate cross sections indicating bioturbation. Scale bar is 2 cm long.

Small-scale faults, oversteepened bedding, and podlike distribution of bedding are common in units 4, 5, and 6. These features are particularly evident along the contact between unit 6 and units 4 and 5 (fig. 30).

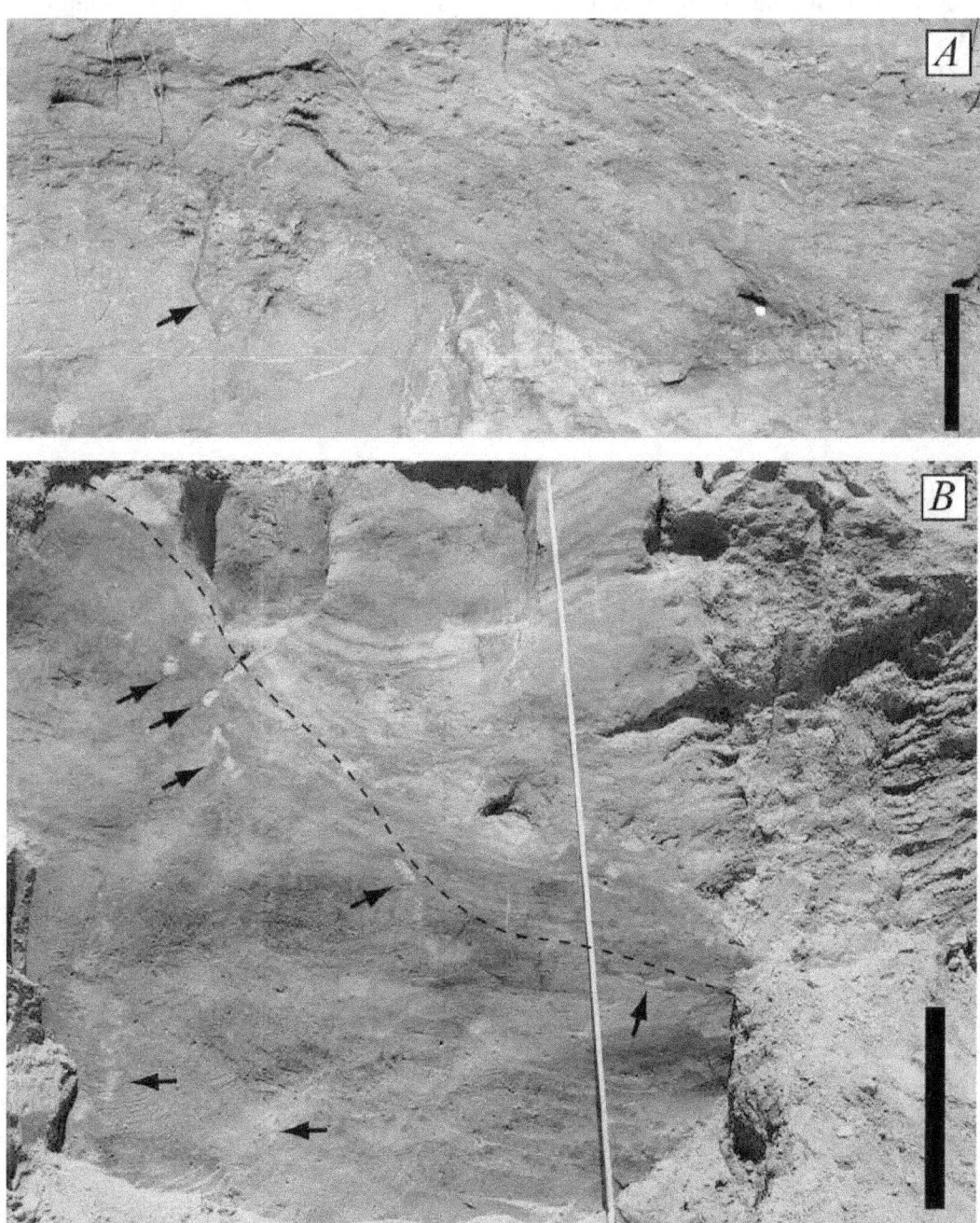

Figure 30. Photographs of soft-sediment deformation attributed to thermokarst in unit 4 and unit 6 at sites 3A and 4B. *A*, Contact between unit 4 and unit 6 at site 3A. Well-bedded sand, pebbly sand, and mud of unit 6 are rotated into a depression caused by faulting and disruption of the underlying unit 4. Note small fault-bounded depression (arrow) in which unit 6 thickens. Scale bar is 40 cm long. *B*, Contact between unit 4 and unit 6 at site 4B. Layering in unit 6 (above dashed line) is rotated to nearly vertical, but layering offlaps contact, suggesting that collapse was synchronous with sedimentation. Circular and ovate sand features (arrows) are interpreted as injection pipes of basal unit 4 sand. Scale bar is 50 cm long.

Thermokarst is commonly accompanied by expulsion of water and abrupt loss of volume (French, 2007, p. 186–215). The soft-sediment features observed in the pit are all consistent with this interpretation, although a seismic origin cannot be ruled out solely on the basis of this exposure. Unit 6 deposits at sites 3A and 4B are rotated along faulted contacts in the underlying unit 4. At site 3A, numerous faults offset small parts to the entire thickness of unit 4 (fig. 31). At site 4B, there are no beds in unit 4 to indicate offset, but the lowest beds of unit 6 are disturbed and faulted where the basal contact is oversteepened to nearly vertical (fig. 32). These features are consistent with the loss of volume accompanying thaw of permafrost during deposition of unit 6. Near site 1B along the northwestern wall, unit 7 (gray silt with thick laminae, fig. 21) appears to be isolated as a pod within gravel and sand similar to the "sediment-filled pots" of French (2008, p. 185). The unit 7 silt appears to be set into deposits of unit 2, but the unit 2 surface could have been an eroded exposure during a time of permafrost development.

Figure 31. Photographs of soft-sediment deformation attributed to thermokarst in unit 4 at sites 3A and 2B. *A*, Small fault offsetting the entire thickness of unit 4 at site 3A. Unit 6 thickens where it overlies the downwarped side, indicating accumulation during deformation. Scale bar is 15 cm long. *B*, Sheet of clean sand (white) with a sharp basal contact is interpreted as an injection sill of lower unit 4 at site 2B. Tube-like projections into the overlying mottled unit 4 (arrows) are interpreted as injection pipes. Note small sill at lower right. Scale bar is 25 cm long.

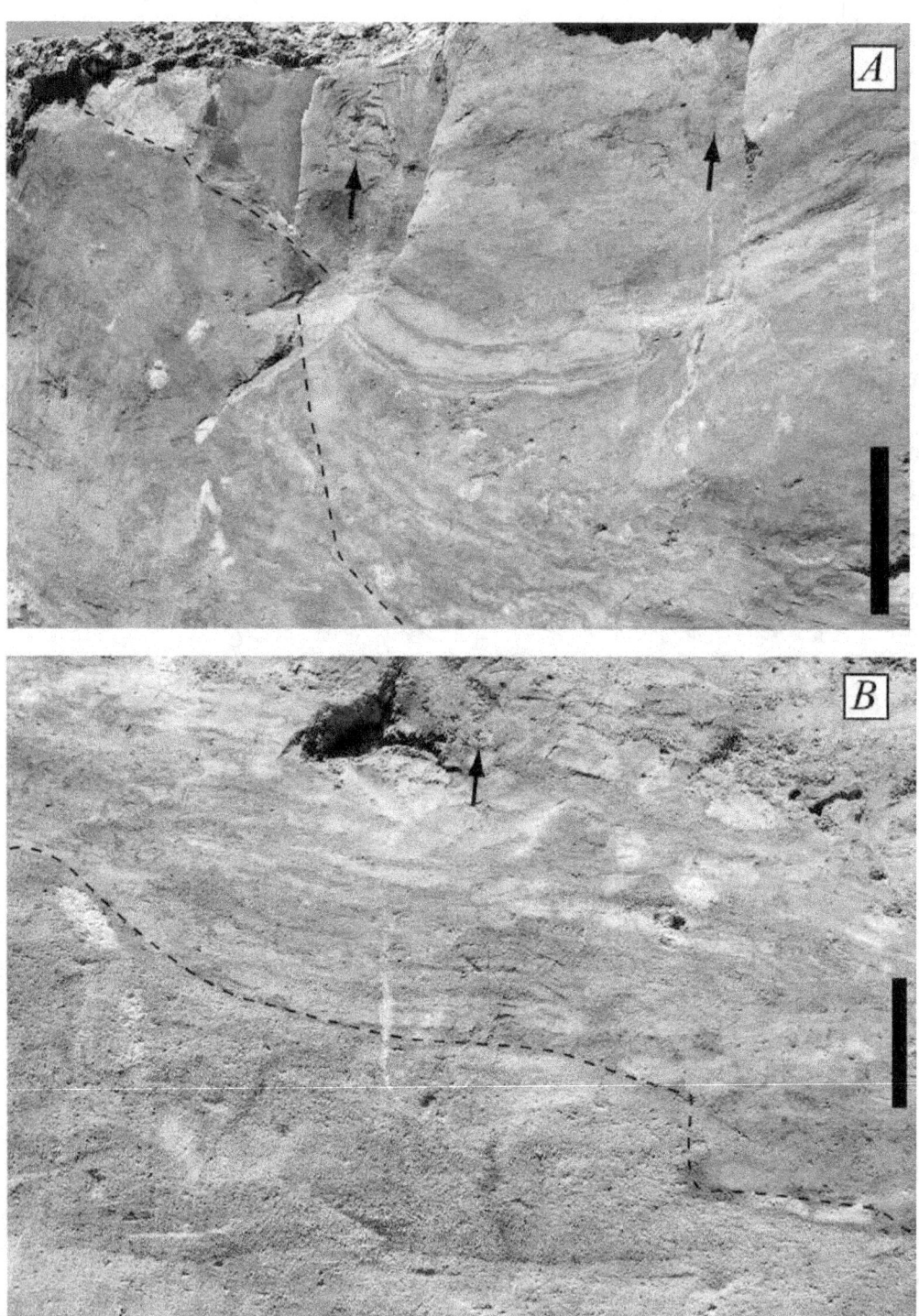

Figure 32. Photographs of soft-sediment deformation attributed to thermokarst in unit 4 and unit 6 at site 4B. *A,* Base of unit 6 (dashed line) on updip edge at site 4B. White circular to ovate features are filled with clean sand and interpreted as injection pipes of lower unit 4. Convoluted beds in upper part of unit 6 (arrows) may be involutions due to freeze-thaw cycles. Scale bar is 30 cm long. *B,* Detail of basal contact of unit 6 at site 4B. Note broken and disrupted sediment immediately above the contact with unit 4 (dashed line). Also note faulting of layers above the contact (arrow). White patches in unit 6 are reduction spots around sandy features that may include the injection pipes. Scale bar is 10 cm long.

Fluid-injection features are also indicated within the units modified by other thermokarst indicators. Cylindrical-sand features filled with material similar to basal unit 4 (fig. 32) crosscut mottled unit 4 at sites 2B and 3B. The cylinders appear to attach to wedge-shaped features with discontinuous wedges of sand following wedge margins. At site 2B, lower unit 4 sand has formed an injection sill within the mottled upper part of unit 4 (fig. 31B). Cylindrical sand pipes extend up from the upper contact and connect to wedge-shaped features, producing discontinuous slivers of sand within them. Near site 1B, some of the tube-shaped features filled with clean sand (fig. 21) may also be injection features.

Another set of features that is consistent with permafrost consists of small-scale deformed beds, isolated pods of sand and mud, and open vugs in sand and silt layers that are attributed to freeze-thaw cycles in the active layer of a frozen soil (Fox and Protz, 1981; Van Vliet-Lanoe and others, 1984; Van Vliet-Lanoe, 1998). Small-scale deformation structures in unit 5 (fig. 12) may be involution features due to freeze-thaw cycles in the active layer. Deformed beds in the uppermost part of unit 6 at site 4B (figs. 32 and 33) are similar to involution structures. The location of these deformation structures immediately below the road surface, however, suggests the possibility that they are due to loading by heavy equipment when the sediment was wet.

Figure 33. Photograph of soft-sediment deformation in the upper part of unit 6 at site 4B. Layered fine sand and mud are deformed into a bowl-like feature with flame-like edges as shown in figure 32A. The deformation style is similar to involutions due to freeze-thaw cycles in the active layer above permafrost. The deformation shown here is restricted to a spot where unit 8 cover is minimal, allowing for deformation by heavy equipment loading. Scale bar is 5 cm long.

Spherical blebs of sand and mud are abundant in upper unit 4 (fig. 34). At site 3A, sand blebs are abundant in association with deformed sand layers resembling nivation features or involution structures. At site 4B, small spherical blebs of orange stain and larger spheres of mud characterize the uppermost part of unit 4. Spherical features of submillimeter size have been attributed to cryogenic soils (Fox and Protz, 1981; Van Vliet-Lanoe and others, 1984), but it is not clear if larger scale features are also produced. Ice crystals in frozen soils produce open vugs and blocky parting (Van Vliet-Lanoe and others, 1984; Van Vliet-Lanoe, 1998; Bray and others, 2006; French, 2008). Blocky vugs consistent with ice crystal morphologies were observed in the uppermost part of unit 4 at site 2B (fig. 35A). At site 4B, the uppermost part of unit 6 has an irregular blocky texture superimposed on the layering (fig. 35B) and there are large flattened vugs that resemble ice-crystal fabrics shown by Bray and others (2006).

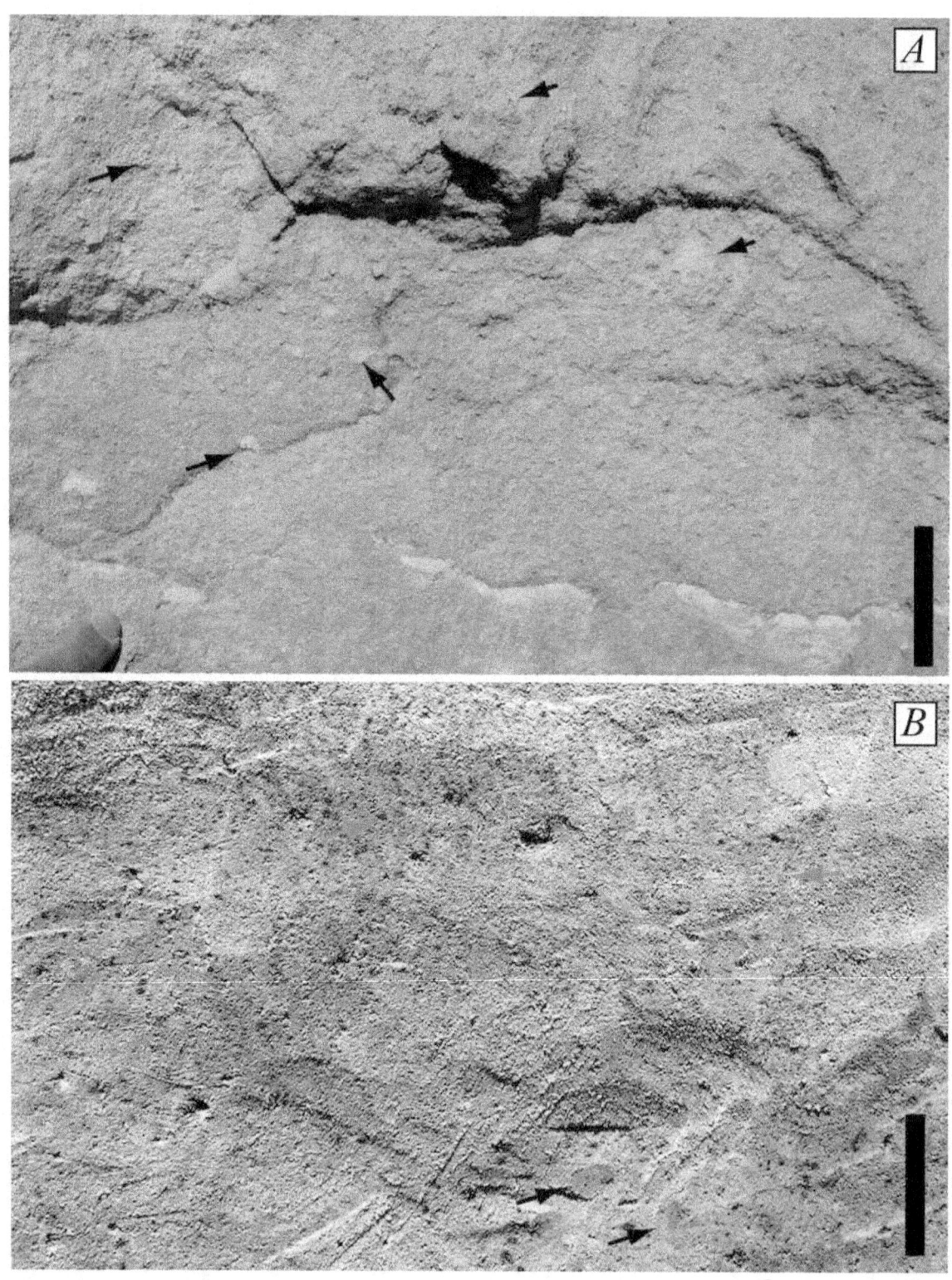

Figure 34. Photographs of spherical sand and mud features in uppermost unit 4 at sites 3A and 4B. *A*, At site 3A, well-sorted sand forms spheres 2 to 10 mm in diameter (arrows). These are associated with deformed beds of well-sorted sand that may be niveo-aeolian deposits. Scale bar is 5 cm long. *B*, At site 4B, spheroidal clumps of silty mud (black arrows) and iron-oxide-cemented sand (red arrows) are scattered in mottled sand. Scale bar is 3 cm long.

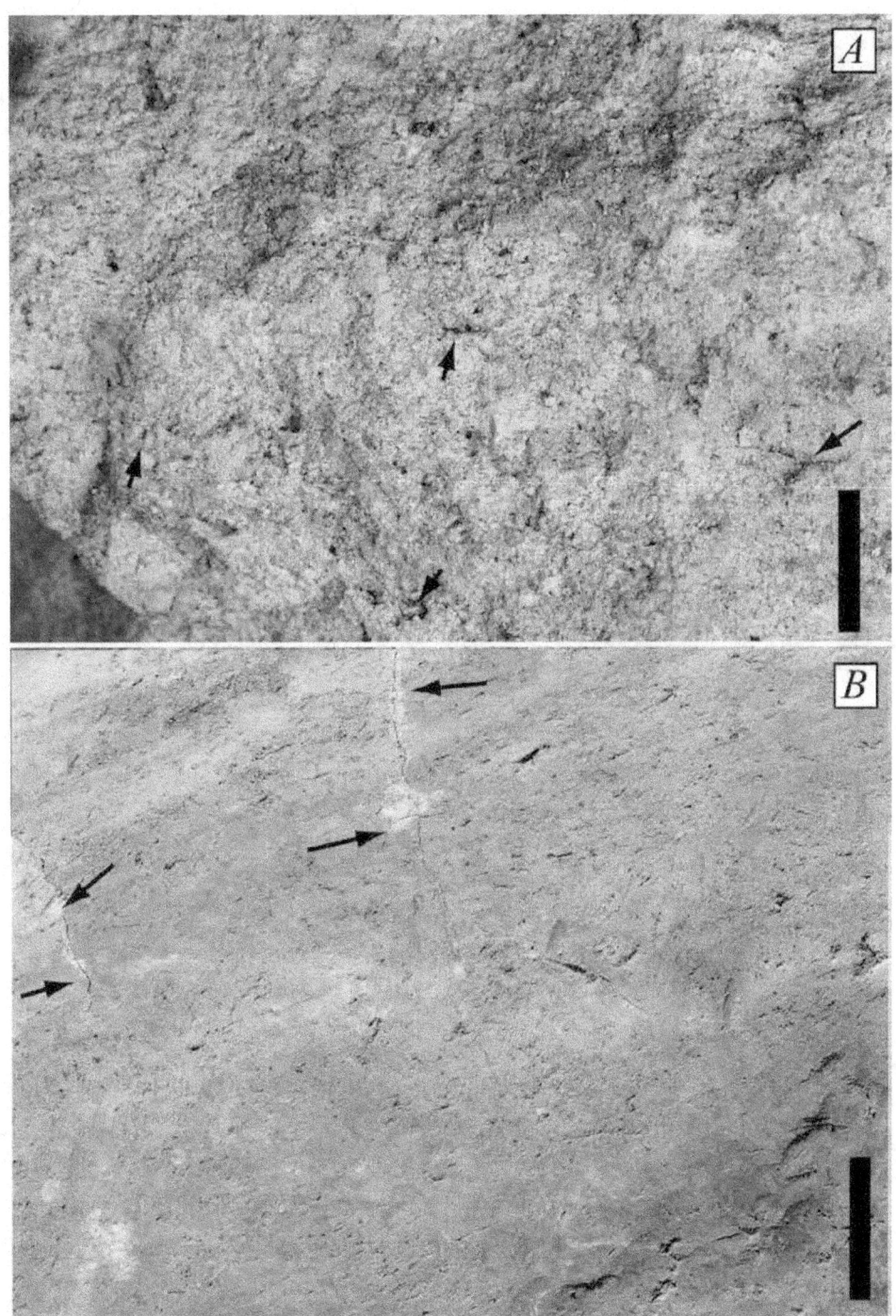

Figure 35. Photographs of open vug features attributed to former ice crystals in unit 4 at site 2B and unit 6 at site 4B. *A*, Hand sample of unit 4 at site 2B containing spherical segregations of sand and mud and numerous blocky open vugs (arrows) that range from 0.5 to 2 mm in width. Scale bar is 2 cm long. *B*, Cleaned surface of uppermost unit 6 at site 4B showing flattened vugs (dark areas) and irregular mottling of interbedded fine sand and mud. This part of unit 6 had a platy parting character absent in similar bedding lower in the unit. Note clean white sand features (arrows) that partially follow cracks. Scale bar is 2 cm long.

Geometry of Sedimentary Units

The interpretations of vertical distributions of the different sedimentary units are based on observations at the sites where the outcrop was cleaned (figs. 36–42). The lateral distribution of some units could be physically traced along the pit walls, whereas others are inferred from our assessment of the units present at isolated localities. In general, the northeastern wall provided the best continuous exposure, and direct observations were made of the distribution of units 1, 2, 3, 4, and 7 over the northern two-thirds of its length (fig. 2). Observations on the southern third of the northeastern wall were limited to the 2007 reconnaissance study because that part of the outcrop was leveled by 2008.

Different parts of the northwestern wall of the pit were cleaned in 2007 and 2008, and so direct observations of unit relationships were not possible. Unit 7 provides a distinct marker to infer lateral associations, but the certainty is lower than for the northeastern wall.

The southwestern wall of the pit was uncapped to provide sediment for the adjacent landfill mound (fig. 24); it was mostly composed of unit 1. Overlying deposits were only patchily exposed so that lateral relationships must be inferred from the interpretation of each unit. A thick cap of unit 8 representing a roadbed running along that wall dominated the southeastern wall of the pit. Small portions of unit 1 and unit 2 were intermittently exposed.

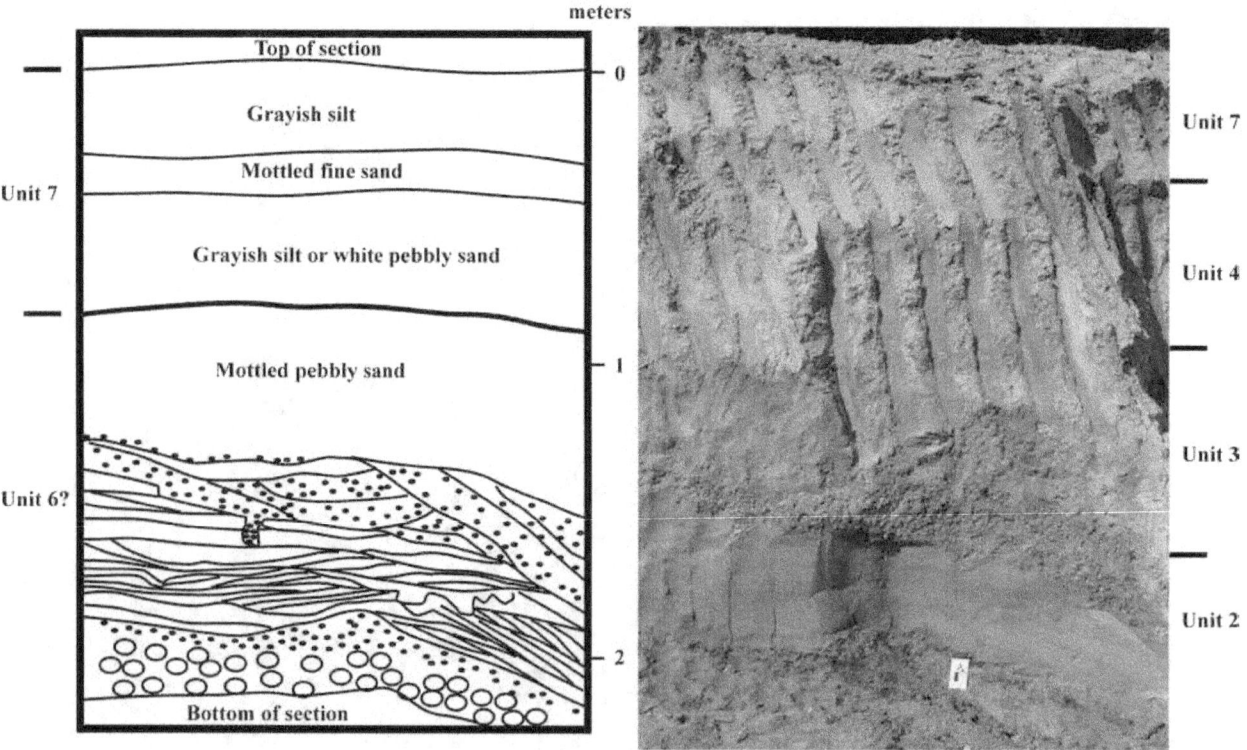

Figure 36. Sketch and photograph of site 1A. Two interpretations of the units at this site are provided. The lower part of the photograph is equivalent to figure 17. The explanation on the left side of the sketch interprets the lower part of the exposure as unit 6 and the overlying light-gray unit as a silt. The explanation on the right side of the photograph requires that the first light-colored unit be a pebbly sand. The latter succession is more consistent with observations elsewhere in the pit, but it implies that soft-sediment deformation features are present in unit 2. The soft-sediment deformation features may have formed without influence by ice.

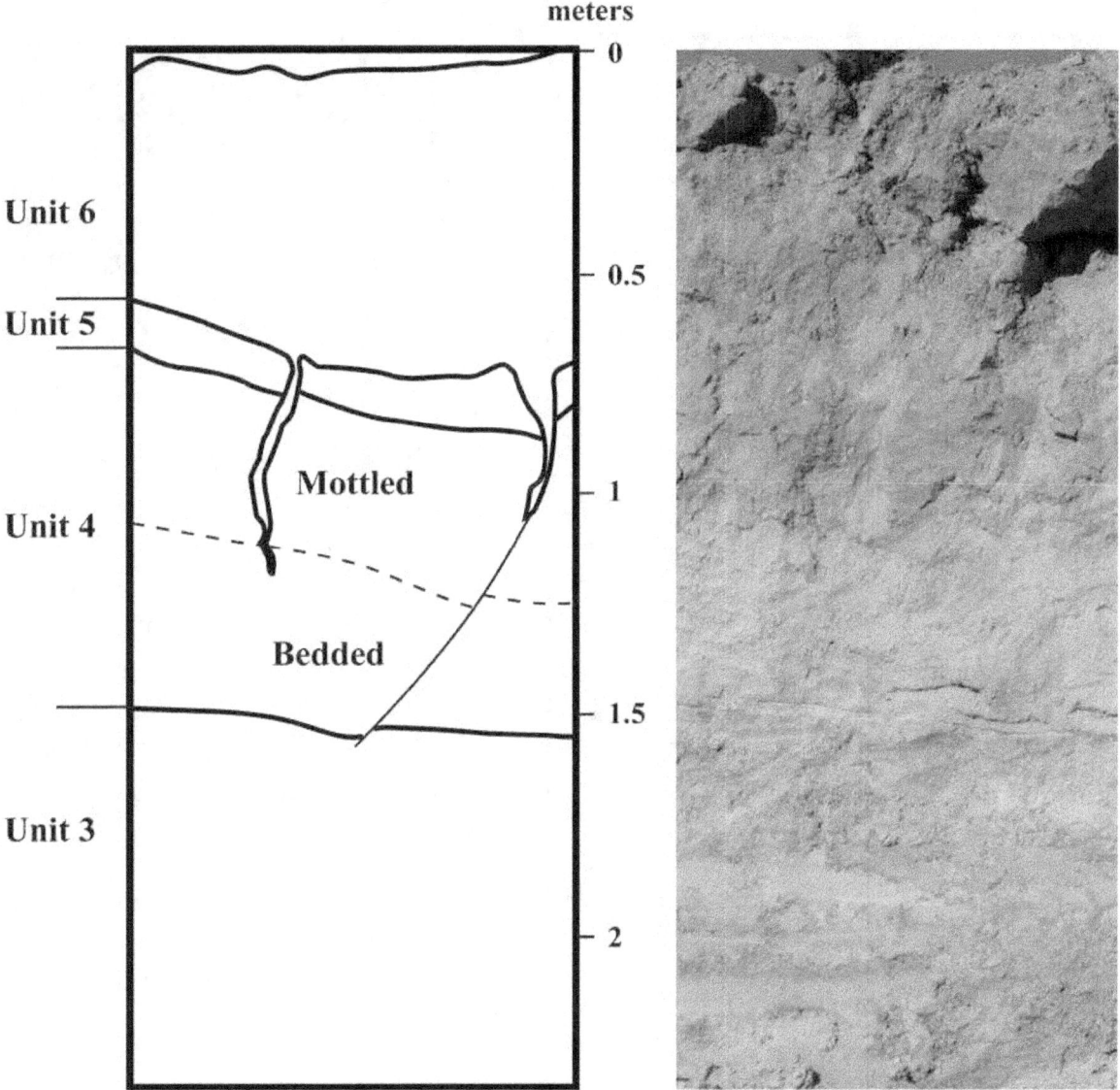

Figure 37. Sketch and photograph of site 3A. Note faulting of unit 4 and thickening of unit 6 over the downdropped side. Dashed line indicates approximate transition from preserved bedding in unit 4 to mottled with orange stains. Positions of wedge-shaped features are shown. Bedding-like features in lower part of unit 3 are backhoe tool marks.

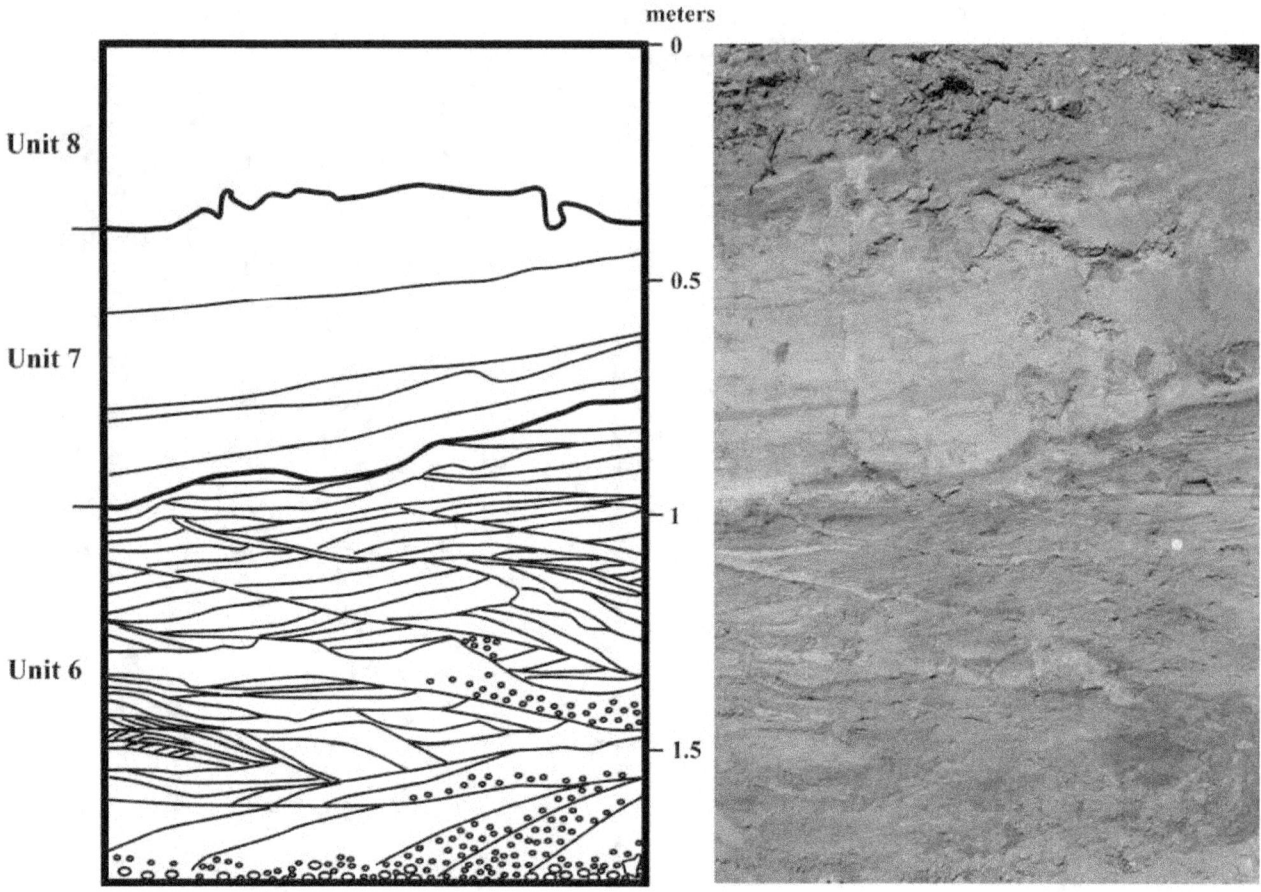

Figure 38. Sketch and photograph of site 4A. Note multiple bedding bands in unit 7 defined by alternations of sand-rich and silt-rich horizons. Upper contact with unit 8 is broken and disturbed. Lower part of unit 6 is partially covered by loose debris.

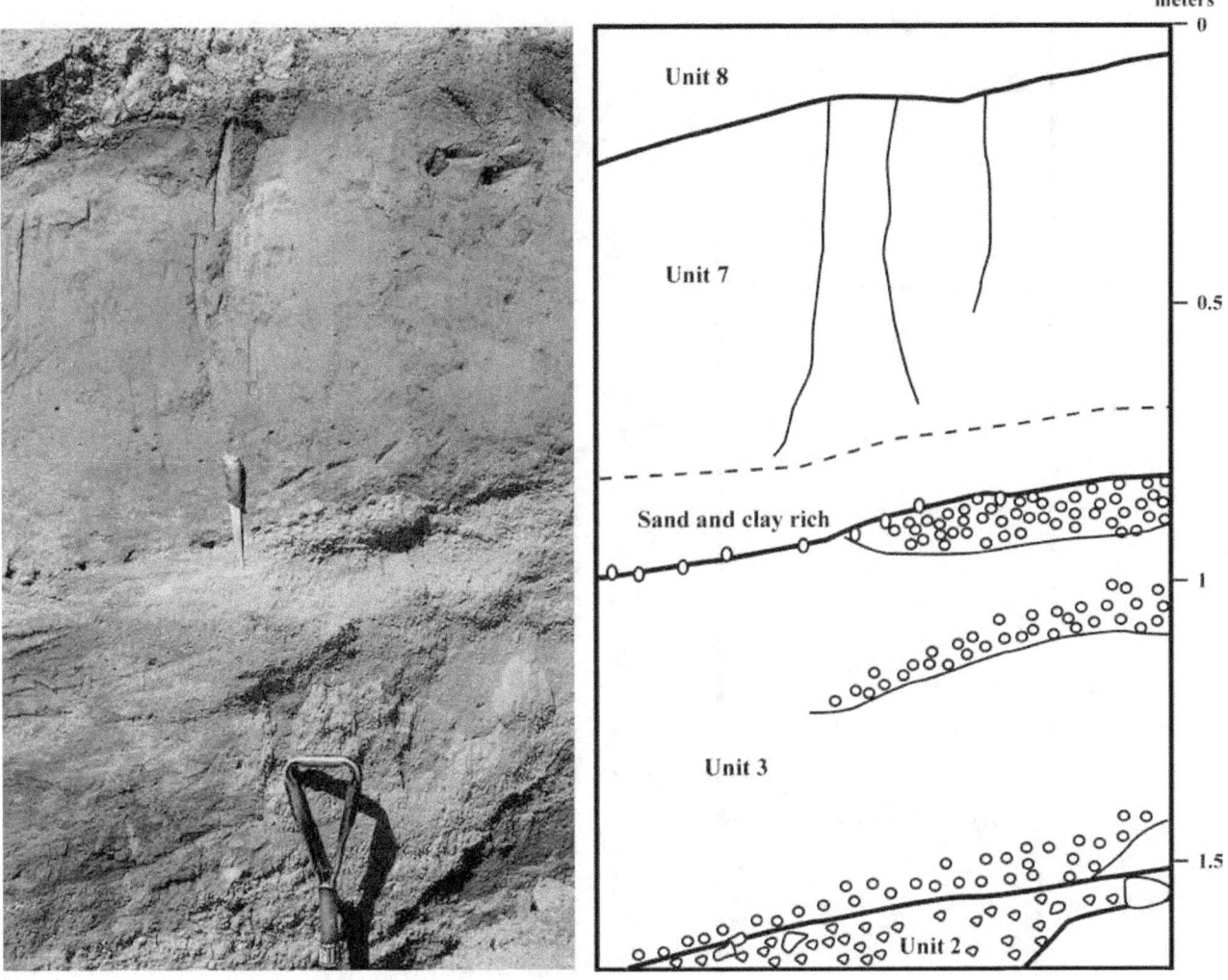

Figure 39. Sketch and photograph of site 1B. Locations of vertical crack planes in unit 7 are shown. Dashed line shows approximate contact between mottled sand and mud at the base of unit 7 and the more typical silt above. Pebble beds of unit 3 are shown. The conglomerate assigned to unit 2 at the base could also be part of unit 3.

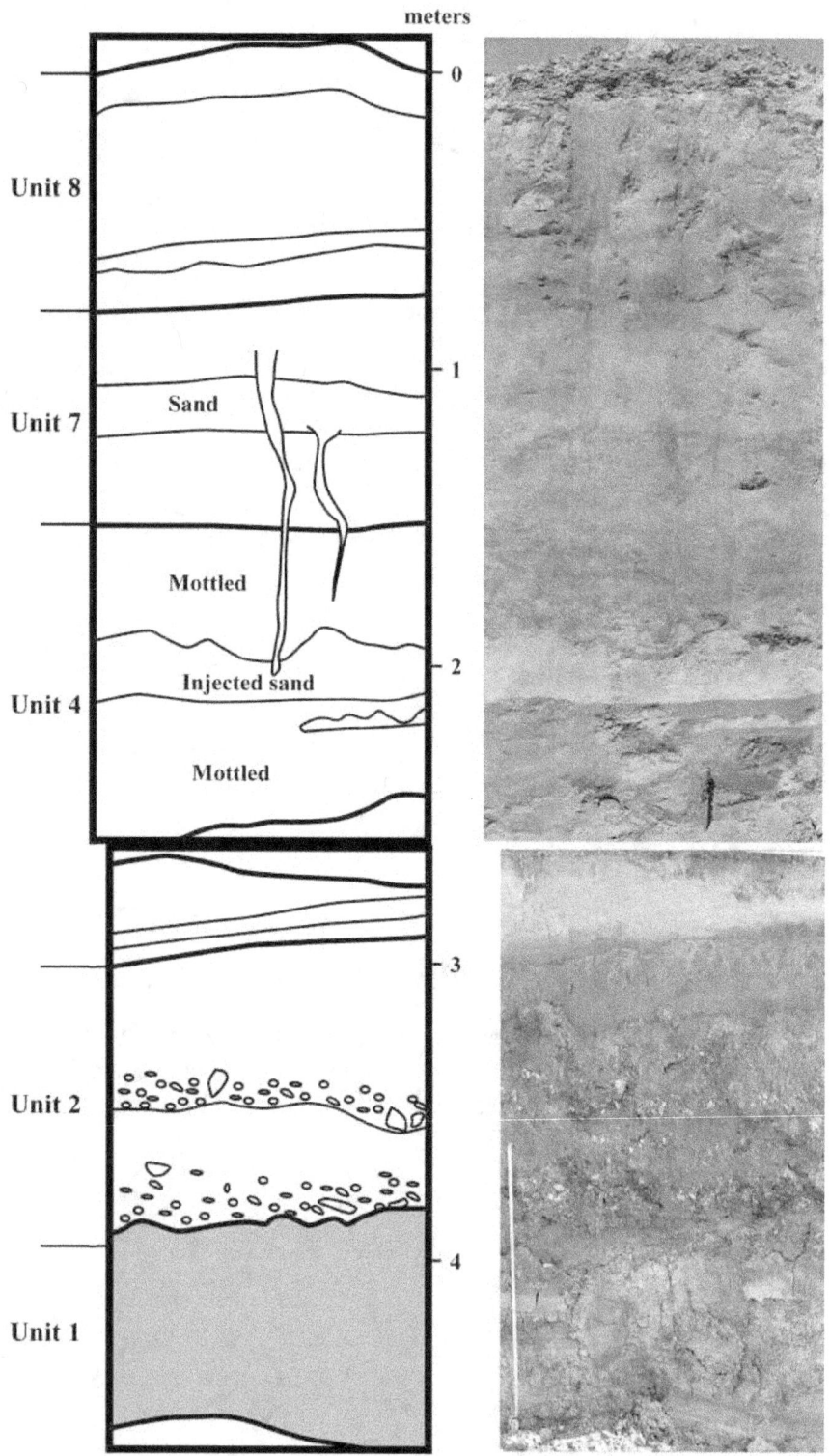

Figure 40. Sketch and photographs of site 2B. Lower part of section is a separate exposure about 2 m in front of the upper part of the section. The top of the lower section was projected onto the upper section using a level. The lowermost part of unit 4 has bedding features and the upper part is split by two injected sheets of white sand. The two layers of unit 7 are separated by a thin orange-stained sand. The locations of the largest wedge-shaped features are shown.

56

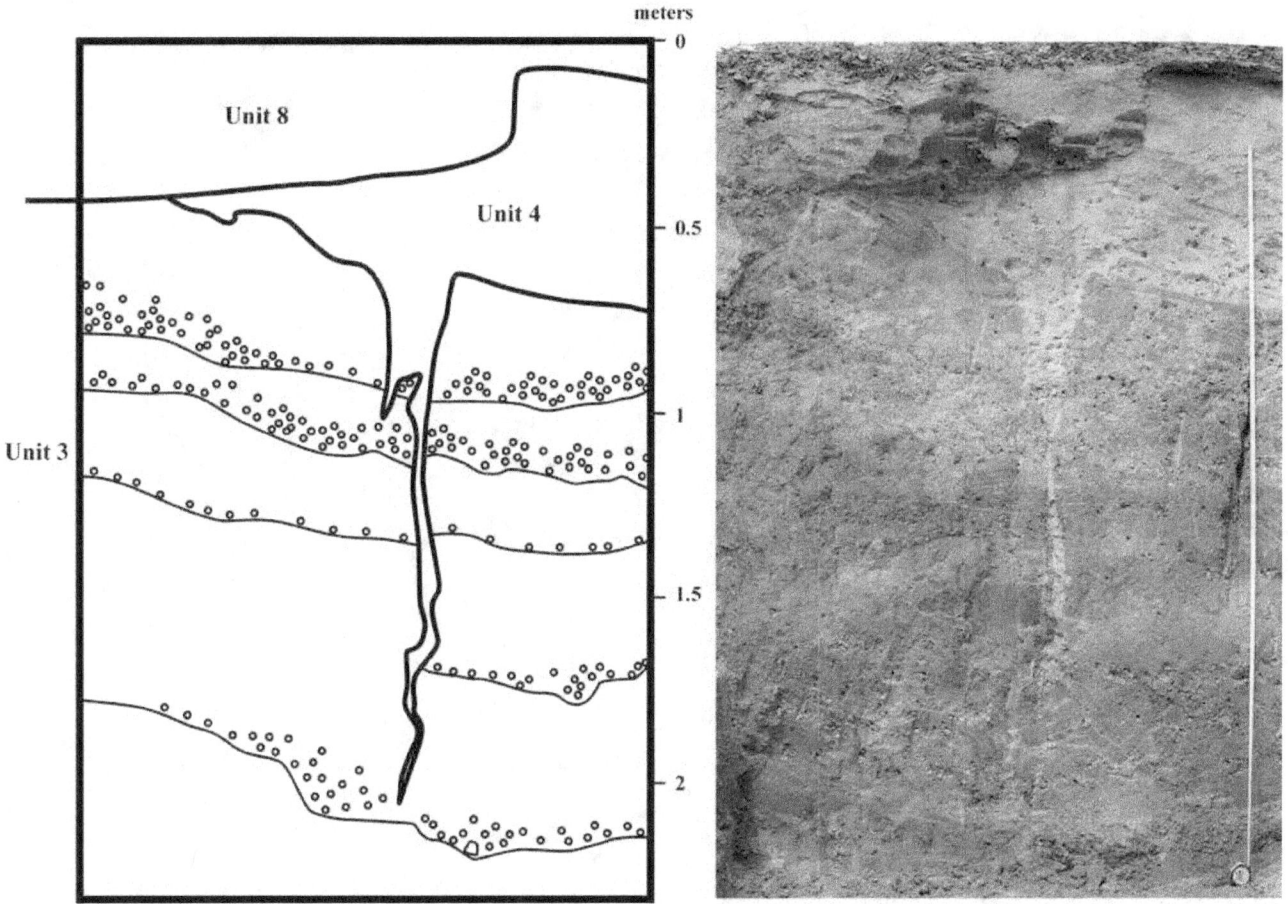

Figure 41. Sketch and photograph of site 3B. Note inclination of the contact between unit 3 and unit 4. Location of large wedge structure through unit 4 and unit 3 is shown. Coarsest pebble layers in unit 3 are also shown. The remainder of the unit is mottled sandy mud.

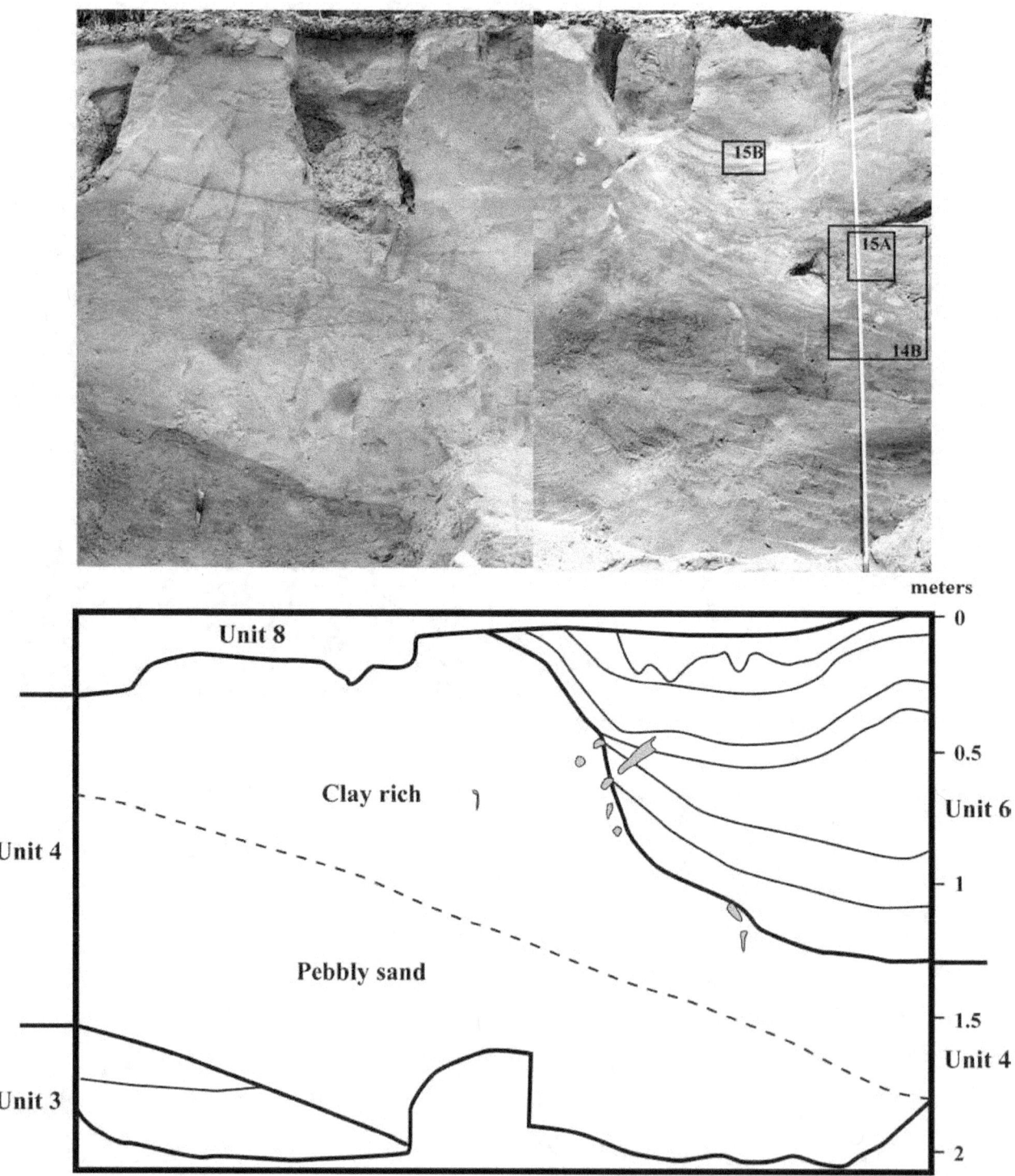

Figure 42. Sketch and photographs of site 4B. The left and right parts of the exposure were cleaned and photographed on different days. The locations of the largest sand-filled injection pipes are shown (gray in sketch). Dashed line shows the boundary between burrow-mottled pebbly sand and clay-rich mottled sand. Contact between units 3 and 4 is actually below the color break in the left side of picture. Bowl-shaped depressions in the upper part of exposure are erosional gullies partially filled with unit 8. Locations of areas shown in figures 14B, 15A, and 15B are indicated by boxes.

Figure 43 illustrates the lateral distribution of the different sedimentary units along the northeastern and northwestern walls of the pit. Unit 1 uniformly underlies the entire area, but the upper surface has as much as a meter of vertical relief from erosion before deposition of unit 2. Unit 2 is thickest in the central part of the pit, which was also the area of highest relief before the pit was excavated (fig. 2). Unit 2 also thins towards the southwest, but this thinning is mostly due to removal of material during excavation. Unit 2 is mostly cobble conglomerate where exposures are thin but includes crossbedded pebbly sand and multiple erosional surfaces where it is thicker.

Unit 3 has a distribution similar to unit 2, but it may be absent from the southwestern side of the pit. Conglomerate beds separated by a sand with tabular foresets at site 1A (fig. 17) are shown as part of unit 2 overlain by unit 3 and a relatively thin section of unit 4. The crossbedding in the sand layer resembles reactivation surfaces on a tidal bar, suggesting that it could be unit 6. It is not known if the basal light-colored unit overlying it is pebbly sand or silt. In the latter case, it is more likely that the conglomerate and sand and the mottled pebbly sand are all part of unit 6, forming a local channel fill.

Unit 4 is thickest at site 4B and is less than a meter thick elsewhere in its exposure. Unit 5 was observed only at site 3A, although spherical coarse sand blebs were found in the upper part of unit 4 at site 4B.

Unit 6 forms a series of lenses cut into the older units. It is thickest and sandiest at site 4A. An open-framework pebble conglomerate with muddy interbeds at site 5B is interpreted as unit 6 overlying unit 2, but its actual stratigraphic position is unknown. Unit 6 is absent from sites 3B and 2B, although 4- to 10-m-wide lenses of it were visible on unprepared surfaces between these sites. At site 1B, a mottled sand and gray mud directly below typical silt of unit 7 could be a thin remnant of unit 4 or unit 6.

Unit 7 is visible even on unprepared surfaces as a sheetlike continuous unit. It is missing from sites 3B and 4B and the southwestern pit wall. These absences could be due to removal of material during earlier construction of the roads and excavation of the pit.

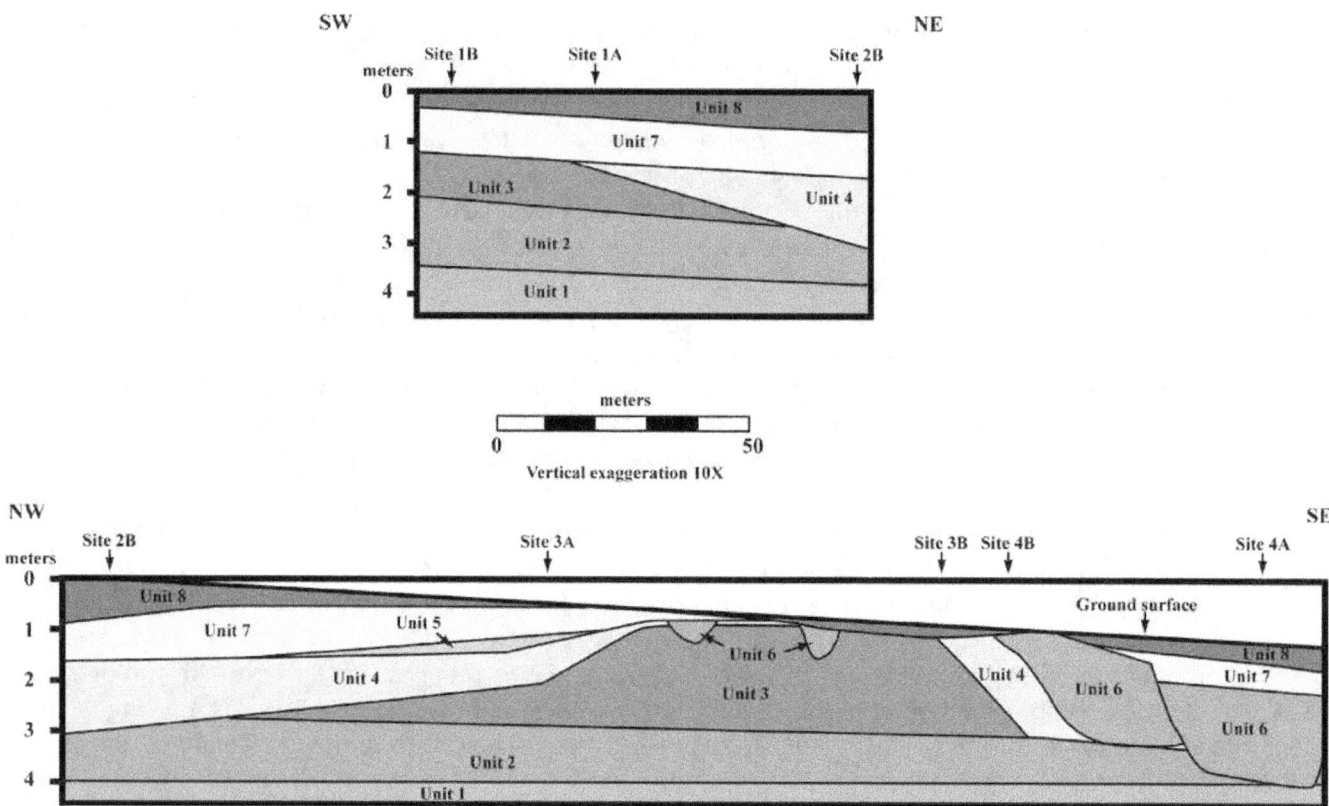

Figure 43. Cross sections showing lateral distribution of sedimentary units along the northwestern wall (upper) and the northeastern wall (lower) of the Midshore Regional Solid Waste Facility pit. The correlation in the northwestern wall reflects the assumption that the conglomerate and sand at the base of site 1A are part of unit 2 rather than unit 6. The locations of unit 6 channel scours between sites 3A and 3B in the northeastern wall are approximate. Note the vertical exaggeration. The dip of the unit 4 basal contact on the southeast side of the northeastern wall is actually about 10 degrees.

Depositional Model

This section discusses the possible depositional environments and ages of units 1 through 8 at the Midshore Regional Solid Waste Facility near Easton, MD. The interpretations and possible correlative formation names are summarized in table 1.

Table 1. Formation name, depositional environment, and age of units 1 through 8 studied at the Midshore Regional Solid Waste Facility near Easton, MD.

[ka, thousand years before present]

Unit number	Formation	Depositional environment	Age
8	Artificial fill	Road building and pit excavation.	Modern
		Permafrost development and soil overprint	
7	Parsonsburg Sand or a younger unnamed unit.	Wetland accumulating windblown silt from glacier-derived material.	30 ka to 13 ka or younger than 10,500 B.C.
6	Kent Island Formation	Marine transgression up the ancestral Choptank River valley during a warming period that melted the permafrost layer in units 3 and 4.	Marine isotope stages 5e to 3, between 120 ka and 30 ka.
5	Unnamed	Accumulation of niveo-aeolian sediment over snow.	Younger than unit 4
		Subaerial exposure and formation of permafrost	
4	Unnamed	Marine transgression up the ancestral Choptank River valley.	Close in age to the Omar Formation, which was deposited at 225 ka in marine isotope stage 7.
3	Unnamed	Colluvial fans of small drainages off highland underlain by unit 2.	Late Pliocene, younger than the Beaverdam Formation.
2	Pensauken Formation	High-energy braided-river system.	Late Miocene to Pliocene
1	Choptank Formation	Shallow marine shelf	Miocene

Units 1 and 2 are interpreted as Tertiary deposits similar to those underlying the highlands in the surrounding area. Unit 1 is interpreted as the Choptank Formation representing shallow-shelf sedimentation during the Miocene. During the latest Miocene or the Pliocene, a high-energy braided-river system cut through the early Tertiary marine sequences and deposited the sand and gravel of unit 2, the Pensauken Formation. River flow was from the north in the pit section, although clasts in the Pensauken indicate a source area that could have come anywhere from the west to the northeast from the Piedmont and Appalachians.

Although unit 3 could be a lateral facies of unit 2, it is interpreted here as colluvial and alluvial deposits of small drainages off the nearby highland underlain by unit 2. Newell and Clark (2008) indicated that during the late Pliocene, the Beaverdam Formation was "inset" into the Pensauken Formation in nearby Worcester County, MD, based on the maps and reports of Owens and Denny (1979, 1986). Deposition of the Beaverdam Formation probably occurred during the initial formation of the Choptank River valley and the development of local relief allowing deposition of unit 3. The sediments were deposited by small streams draining primarily to the southeast, probably as colluvial fans. The surfaces of the fans were vegetated, producing the mottled fabric of soil development that is characteristic of this unit.

Unit 4 contains sediment representing a marine terrace-cutting event overlain by nearshore sand and fine gravel. In Worcester County, Newell and Clark (2008) identified marine sands overlying terraces at an elevation of less than 10 m that they assigned to the Omar Formation of Owens and Denny (1986). This elevation is close to that of unit 4 but appears to be lower. The Omar Formation is currently interpreted as equivalent to marine isotope stage 7 highstand (Newell and Clark, 2008) at about 225 ka. The terrace front in this study area dips to the southeast, and the sand thins towards the northwest. These characteristics are consistent with a marine transgression up the ancestral Choptank River valley. The absence of unit 4 on the southwestern side of the pit may indicate that it was higher than the marine transgression at that time or that the deposits were subsequently eroded.

After deposition, unit 4 was extensively modified by soil processes and permafrost. The heavily mottled upper bedding surface with a clay-rich matrix is attributed to soil development following a drop in sea level. Permafrost conditions are indicated by the well-developed wedges and inferred from the unusual spherical sand segregations found in the uppermost portions. The upper part of unit 3 was also modified by permafrost.

Unit 5 is interpreted as a deposit formed during the time unit 4 was receiving a permafrost overprint. Unit 5 is either a surface with grain-size segregation due to freezing and thawing or it represents an accumulation of niveo-aeolian sediment over a semipermanent snow cover.

Unit 6 indicates another rise of sea level along the Choptank River valley. The southeastern part of the pit was within a major channel that experienced strong tidal exchange producing the crossbedding sequence at site 4A and the open-framework gravels with mud drapes at site 5B. The smaller scale lenses in the northwestern part of the pit are interpreted as sinuous channels draining the highlands to the northwest. This interpretation would also explain the coarse-grained nature of the channel fill in association with the intercalation of fine sand and mud. Deposition of unit 6 began with a warming period that melted the permafrost layer in units 3 and 4. The deposition of at least the smaller channels appears to have been synchronous with dewatering and collapse of the permafrost on unit 4 (thermokarst). The timing of lower terrace formation, including the Kent Island Formation, has been dated within the range of marine isotope stages 5e to 3 (Owens and Denny, 1979) or somewhere between 120 ka and 30 ka. Unit 6 was probably also formed during that time period.

Unit 7 is interpreted as having formed during another cold, dry period with aeolian sedimentation. Angular silt-sized grains and clay-sized material nearly devoid of clay minerals suggest deposition as windblown silt from glacier-derived material. The windblown sediment accumulated on a surface that was covered with shallow water or a wetland that supported vegetation. This surface may have dried out intermittently and allowed accumulation of sand and the formation of desiccation cracks.

Permafrost conditions produced wedges that initiated in unit 7 and penetrated into unit 4 (fig. 40). If the deformed bedding features at the top of unit 6 at site 4B are involution structures rather than features caused by heavy equipment (fig. 33), they suggest that permafrost conditions predated deposition of unit 7 locally. If the unusual sand deposits at site 4A are not unit 6, then it is possible that unit 7 actually predates unit 6. In this case, the deposits would reflect only one episode of permafrost feature development. Suggestions of thermokarst development following deposition of unit 7 include the lens of laminated unit 7 at site 1B and the possible sand pipes connecting to wedges in unit 7.

If unit 7 is equivalent to the Parsonsburg Sand (Denny and others, 1979), it may represent deposition spanning 30 ka to 13 ka. Wah (2003) constrained the age of the Delmarva Quaternary silt blanket by noting the age of an archeological site about 35 km southeast of the Midshore Regional Solid Waste Facility. On Tilghman Island, an archeological site contained projectile points indicating an age of 10,500 B.C. overlain by a meter-thick silt bed. If unit 7 is equivalent to those deposits, it could be younger than 10,500 years. The soil fabrics with carbonized roots in the upper part of unit 7 at sites 1B and 2B are younger than the wedges attributed to permafrost. The soil development may be much younger than the silt deposit.

Unit 8 is interpreted as artificial fill related to the operation of the Midshore Regional Solid Waste Facility and excavation of the pit.

References Cited

Bray, M.T., French, H.M., and Shur, Y., 2006, Further cryostratigraphic observations in the CRREL Permafrost Tunnel, Fox, Alaska: Permafrost and Periglacial Processes, v. 17, no. 3, p. 233–243.

Bridge, J.S., and Demicco, R.V., 2008, Earth surface processes, landforms and sediment deposits: Cambridge, U.K., Cambridge University Press, Cambridge, 830 p.

Cailleux, A., 1978, Niveo-aeolian deposits, *in* Fairbridge, R.W., and Bourgeois, Joanne, eds., The encyclopedia of sedimentology, v. 6 *of* Encyclopedia of Earth Sciences: Stroudsburg, Pa., Dowden, Hutchinson, & Ross, p. 501–503.

Demicco, R.V., and Hardie, L.A., 1994, Sedimentary structures and early diagenetic features of shallow marine carbonate deposits: SEPM Atlas Series, no. 1, 265 p.

Denny, C.S., and Owens, J.P., 1979, Sand dunes on the central Delmarva Peninsula, Maryland and Delaware: U.S. Geological Survey Professional Paper 1067–C, 15 p.

Denny, C.S., Owens, J.P., Sirkin, L.A., and Rubin, Meyer, 1979, The Parsonsburg Sand in the central Delmarva Peninsula, Maryland and Delaware: U.S. Geological Survey Professional Paper 1067–B, 16 p.

Dijkmans, J.W.A., 1990, Niveo-aeolian sedimentation and resulting sedimentary structures; Sondre Stromfjord area, western Greenland: Permafrost and Periglacial Processes, v. 1, no. 2, p. 83–96.

Fox, C.A., and Protz, R., 1981, Definition of fabric distributions to characterize the rearrangement of soil particles in the turbic cryosols: Canadian Journal of Soil Science, v. 61, no. 1, p. 29–34.

French, H.M., 2007, The periglacial environment (3d ed.): Chichester, England, John Wiley and Sons, Ltd., 458 p.

French, H.M., 2008, Recent contributions to the study of past permafrost: Permafrost and Periglacial Processes, v. 19, no. 2, p. 179–194.

French, H.M., Demitroff, Mark, and Forman, S.L., 2003, Evidence for late-Pleistocene permafrost in the New Jersey Pine Barrens (latitude 39° N), eastern USA: Permafrost and Periglacial Processes, v. 14, no. 3, p. 259–274.

French, H.M., Demitroff, Mark, and Forman, S.L., 2005, Evidence for late-Pleistocene thermokarst in the New Jersey Pine Barrens (latitude 39° N), eastern USA: Permafrost and Periglacial Processes, v. 16, no. 2, p. 173–186.

French, H.M., Demitroff, Mark, Forman, S.L., and Newell, W.L., 2007, A chronology of late-Pleistocene permafrost events in southern New Jersey, eastern USA: Permafrost and Periglacial Processes, v. 18, no. 1, p. 49–59.

Koster, E.A., and Dijkmans, J.W.A., 1988, Niveo-aeolian deposits and denivation forms, with special reference to the Great Kobuk Sand Dunes, northwestern Alaska: Earth Surface Processes and Landforms, v. 13, no. 2, p. 153–170.

Lewkowicz, A.G., and Young, K.L., 1991, Observations of aeolian transport and niveo-aeolian deposition at three lowland sites, Canadian Arctic Archipelago: Permafrost and Periglacial Processes, v. 2, no. 3, p. 197–210.

Newell, W.L., and Clark, Inga, 2008, Geomorphic map of Worcester County, Maryland, interpreted from a LIDAR-based digital elevation model: U.S. Geological Survey Open-File Report 2008–1005, 34 p., 2 oversize sheets. (Available online at http://pubs.usgs.gov/of/2008/1005/.)

Owens, J.P., and Denny, C.S., 1979, Upper Cenozoic deposits of the central Delmarva Peninsula, Maryland and Delaware: U.S. Geological Survey Professional Paper 1067–A, 28 p.

Owens, J.P., and Denny, C.S., 1986, Geologic map of Talbot County [Maryland]: Baltimore, Maryland Geological Survey, scale 1:62,500.

Shattuck, G.B., 1902, The Miocene Formation of Maryland [abs.]: Science, new ser., v. 15, no. 388, p. 906.

Van Vliet-Lanoe, Brigitte, 1998, Frost and soils: Implications for paleosols, paleoclimates and stratigraphy: Catena, v. 34, p. 157–183.

Van Vliet-Lanoe, Brigitte, Coutard, J.-P., and Pissart, Albert, 1984, Structures caused by repeated freezing and thawing in various loamy sediments; A comparison of active, fossil and experimental data: Earth Surface Processes and Landforms, v. 9, no. 6, p. 553–565.

Wah, J.S., 2003, The origin and pedogenic history of Quaternary silts on the Delmarva Peninsula in Maryland: College Park, Md., University of Maryland, unpub. Ph.D. thesis, 271 p.

Weimer, R.J., Howard, J.D., and Lindsay, D.R., 1982, Tidal flats, in Scholle, P.A., and Spears, D.R., eds. Sandstone depositional environments: American Association of Petroleum Geologists Memoir 31, p. 191–245.